The Vatican, the Law and the Human Embryo

By Michael J. Coughlan

D1711634

University of Iowa Press, Iowa City

Contents

Preface		vii
1	Introduction	1
	Catholic and universal	1
	Inalienable human rights	3
	Embryos, human beings, and persons	7
	Conclusions	9
2	Mediation and Saint Thomas Aquinas	11
	Salvation through mediation	11
	Body and soul	17
	Knowledge of the natural law	20
	The influence of Thomas	23
3	What Price Human Life?	26
	Dubious headlines	27
	Double-effect and the Pauline principle	28
	Irreconcilable commitments	31
	The price of human life	35
	The inevitable conclusion	41
4	Natural and Divine Values	42
	Revelation and knowledge of the moral law	42
	Natural law and civil legislation	44
	Church teaching and natural law	45
	Natural law and the special value of human life	49
	Revelation and the special value of human life	53
5	The Argument of the *Instruction*	58
	The concept of a person	59
	The embryo as person?	64
	Souls and embryos	71
	The potentiality argument	74
	Conclusion	76
6	Doubt and Scepticism	78
	The benefit-of-the-doubt argument	78
	Further considerations regarding the concept of a person	80
	The nineteenth-century perspectival change	86

	Doubt and scepticism	88
	'The one who will be a man is already one'	92
7	Revelation and Legislation	97
	The citizen's rights	98
	The embryo/fetus as citizen?	102
	The Christian's dilemma	103
	Justice and equality	107
	Concluding remark: religion, reason, and civil society	111
Notes		113
Bibliography		120
Index		123

Preface

The Warnock Report on human fertilisation and embryology avoided the question whether the human embryo is a person because the answer was regarded as a 'complex amalgam' of factual and moral judgement. Despite this, the Warnock committee felt able to proceed to deal with the question 'how is it right to treat the human embryo'.

This view embodies an attitude which is echoed in a recent ruling of the United States Supreme Court (Webster v. Reproductive Health Services, July 1989) in which the court proceeded to adjudicate on Missouri state legislation on abortion while declining to rule on the preamble to the Missouri statute which claimed that human life begins at conception. The majority opinion was that this was an abstract proposition not relevant to the matters at issue, a view which the *Guardian* correspondent read as implying that it is a question of moral philosophy rather than for law. Concurring with this part of the Supreme Court decision, a leader writer in *The Times* remarked: 'The question of when life and legal rights begin is a matter on which civilised people must agree to differ' (4 July 1989).

Behind this book lies the conviction that this issue cannot be shelved in any of these ways. While not wishing to deny that it is initially a question for moral philosophy, or one which involves a complex amalgam of factual and moral considerations, I believe that it is imperative that we seek to answer it. What is at stake is nothing less than the standing of natural justice.

The Vatican's *Congregation for the Doctrine of the Faith* shares this view. It argues that there must be a detailed reflection on the 'status' of the human embryo before we can begin to deal with the ethical issues raised by artificial procreation and associated biomedical procedures. The Congregation is convinced that, on evidence quite independent of religious beliefs, the conclusion which will follow is that the embryo's status as a person could scarcely be doubted. Thus its treatment as a person is demanded as a matter of natural justice and, therefore, the protection of its right to life is incumbent on civil legislatures of all shades of religious or non-religious persuasion.

The general principles underlying this position are not in

question here. Indeed, as will be seen, they are wholly in accord not only with Catholic tradition but also with an enlightened rational approach to ethics and to legislation. What *is* put in question is how faithfully the principles are being adhered to in recent Church teaching and, in particular, in the 1987 document on artificial procreation techniques. The argument of this book is that the Vatican's teaching on the status of the human embryo rests on flawed rational arguments, bolstered by religious presuppositions. If we rely on the soundest rational arguments alone, we are forced to conclude that the embryo, or early fetus, cannot be considered a person. In consequence, there is no sustainable case for continuing to insist that legislation must protect the embryo or early fetus as a person.

A great deal of ground is covered in this book, much of it barely touched upon here, and much of it at the limits of competence of the author who would have to be a historian, theologian, biologist, and legal theorist, as well as a philosopher, to be fully in command of all aspects. Guidance has been received from colleagues in other relevant disciplines but the book is chiefly that of a moral philosopher taking up the call issued to 'moralists' at the end of the Vatican's instruction on procreation techniques to 'study more deeply' the contents of the Church's teaching. Simultaneously it is a response to the US Court's implied invitation to moral philosophy to take up the question of whether human life begins at conception.

Thanks are due to several colleagues and friends who have helped in many ways with the preparation of this book and most especially to my philosophical critics, R. A. Sharpe and D. A. Cockburn. I am also grateful to Basil Blackwell Ltd and the editors of *Bioethics* for permission to include material from my articles 'Using People', and 'Essential Aims and Unavoidable Responsibilities: A Reply to Anscombe', both in Volume 4 (1990), my review of N. Ford, *When did I begin? Conception of the human individual in history, philosophy and science* in Volume 3 (1989) and '"From the Moment of Conception. . .": The Vatican Instruction on Artificial Procreation Techniques' in Volume 2 (1988).

MICHAEL J. COUGHLAN

1 Introduction

In February of 1987, the Vatican's Congregation for the Doctrine of the Faith published the lengthily entitled document: *Instruction on Respect for Human Life in its Origin and on the Dignity of Procreation* (hereafter, *Instruction*).[1] This constituted the latest and the most comprehensive official response of the Catholic Church to the moral questions being raised by advances in biomedical techniques in the area of human reproduction.

If this document had been offered simply as Church teaching for the consumption of Roman Catholics, then this book would not have been written. However, following a tradition which claims biblical roots and which has been firmly established since the Middle Ages, the Vatican authorities, when dealing with moral and legal issues, speak not only to members of the Church, but to humanity in general, and especially to those responsible for civil legislation (which, in a democratic society, includes every citizen to some degree). The document, therefore, calls for the attention of each and every one of us, Catholic, Protestant, Jew, Muslim, Hindu, agnostic, atheist, or other. It urges upon us values and principles for legislation pertaining to fundamental human rights.

It is the primary aim of this book to assess whether the views it proposes for our acceptance are defensible. This assessment will be made both against a Christian, and especially Catholic, background, and from a non-religious, 'natural philosophy', perspective. Indeed, as will be seen, there is little to differentiate these approaches, as the central Catholic tradition in moral and legal teaching *is* a 'natural philosophy' tradition, that is, it is held to be based on principles universally accessible to human reason and not requiring any special divine revelation. Hence a purely philosophical critique is not only justified, but invited.

CATHOLIC AND UNIVERSAL

From the Catholic point of view, the authoritative status of the document appears to be that of a statement of the 'ordinary Magisterium', that is, of the teaching authority of the Church

1

in a general, but ill-defined, sense. Although it was issued with the express approval of the Pope, this is common practice with the more important publications of this congregation, which is assigned the task of monitoring theological and moral orthodoxy in the Church, and it does not imply that it carries the full weight of papal authority. Certainly it is not being offered as an infallible statement, nor as a final or absolute pronouncement. In accordance with a widely prevalent fashion in Catholic thought, therefore, the *Instruction* may be said to require *religious assent* (the Latin expression is *obsequium*) on the part of the members of the Church, but it is not incumbent upon them to accept it as constituting part of the *substance* of the faith. In pragmatic terms, this appears to mean that, whereas the teaching does not have to be *accepted as true*, it has to be *submitted to in practice*. Catholics might care to note, however, that some of their theologians would place a less demanding interpretation on 'obsequium'.[2]

But, as indicated above, the direct concern of this book lies not with the demands made upon Catholics, *as* Catholics, but with the prescriptions which are set out for the attention of *all* those responsible for public policy, irrespective of religious or political persuasion. The document sets down ethical guidelines on the treatment to be accorded human embryos and on the whole gamut of procreation techniques, from artificial insemination to surrogate motherhood. While divine revelation and established Church teaching are among the bases offered for these guidelines, at least some of the more significant elements are also said to rest upon principles held to stand independently of Catholic teaching. These principles are identified as the 'fundamental moral values' of 'the inviolable right to life of every innocent human individual and the rights of the family and of the institution of marriage', values which are also 'constitutive elements of civil society and its order' (ch. III, p. 35).

From this wider perspective, the document sets its sights beyond appeal to Catholic conscience. Numerous injunctions are directed to the civil powers: 'The political authority is bound to. . .', 'Civil law cannot. . .', 'Legislation must also prohibit. . .', 'It is part of the duty of the public authority to. . .', 'Politicians must commit themselves. . .' (ch. III, p. 37). As such calls are addressed to civil authorities without regard to either the existence of, or the direction of, any religious allegiance, they demand a persuasive defence which does not need to rest on any interpretation of divine revelation, if those civil authorities are to be expected to take cognisance of them. The legitimacy of this demand has traditionally been recognised by the Catholic Church. Indeed, this recognition is firmly embedded in the 'mediation theology', as I have called it, which is the distinctive feature of Catholic thinking in contrast to the mainstream of traditional Protestant thought.

In Chapter 2, the roots and the implications of this focus on mediation are scrutinised. This will require particular attention to be given to the thought of Saint Thomas Aquinas, for reasons which will be explained. The foundation for the rest of the book will be laid in this chapter, for this exposition will indicate to us both the approach which the Church, if it is being faithful to its tradition, ought to be adopting, and, at the same time, what the non-Catholic legislator (or mere citizen) ought to be able to expect when confronted by a document such as the *Instruction*.

INALIENABLE HUMAN RIGHTS

Turning back to the *Instruction*, we find that the injunctions addressed to the civil powers are presented as binding in virtue of their basis in certain 'inalienable human rights'. These rights are identified as:

(a) every human being's right to life and physical integrity from the moment of conception until death; and
(b) the rights of the family and of marriage as an institution and, in this area, the child's right to be conceived, brought into the world and brought up by his parents.

(ch. III, p. 36)

While the first of these rights is almost universally professed to be acknowledged, its implications are a matter of rather less consensus. Both inside and outside the Church, affirmation of this right has accompanied an acceptance of the justice of killing in a number of circumstances (e.g. self-defence, capital punishment, just war), and of the permissibility, under special conditions, of allowing individuals to die when they could be saved (passive euthanasia). This will seem paradoxical only if the right is construed as *absolute*, or, as it is more commonly put, human life is possessed of *absolute value*, or demands *absolute respect*. Yet, as will be seen in Chapter 3, this is precisely how the right is frequently portrayed, not only in popular presentations of Catholicism, but also in official Catholic teaching, particularly in documents relating to the status of embryonic and fetal human life. It will be shown that such unsophisticated construals of the right to life cannot be accepted at face value.

Although this work concentrates on evaluating the Church's case for demanding civil recognition of the right to life of the embryo from conception, a few remarks on the claims made regarding familial rights of the child are apposite here. As in the instance of the right to life, although it might be the case that the rights of the family and of marriage as an institution receive widespread recognition, it is likely that it will be much more difficult to find consensus when the discussion turns to the detailed interpretation of these rights. Do they include the right of a child to be conceived, brought into the world and brought up by *the same couple*? At other points in the document this right is expressed as 'the child's right to be conceived and brought into the world in marriage and from marriage' and the right to 'his filial relationship with his parental origins' (ch. II, sect. 2, p. 24).

This right is said to be violated by the use of surrogate motherhood arrangements and by 'techniques used to obtain a human conception artificially by the use of gametes (i.e. sperm or ova) coming from at least one donor other than the spouses who are joined in marriage' (ch. II, prologue, p. 22n). Artificial insemination by donor, and the use of donated gametes for *in vitro* fertilisation are the most typical of these techniques. In the *Instruction*, these are described as 'heterologous' artificial fertilisation techniques. They are to be contrasted with 'homologous' artificial fertilisation techniques in which gametes of the marriage partners only are employed.

The call for recognition of a right to be *conceived* in defined circumstances poses a conceptual puzzle, for it appears to imply that rights are held by those who do not yet exist. But, let us suppose that this difficulty can be resolved (as suggested by, for example, R. M. Hare[3]). It is unimaginable that a state could or should legislate for the inalienability of the familial rights ascribed to the child in the *Instruction*, if that is understood as making such rights absolute, so that no circumstances may justify overriding them. The obstacles to legislation extend beyond any of the considerations addressed in the *Instruction*. If such legislation were passed, it would, for example, become illegal for natural parents to agree to the adoption of their child; it would place an obligation on parents to care, in the family setting, for the most severely handicapped child irrespective of the consequences for themselves, for the child, or for others; and it would make conceiving an illegitimate child a criminal offence.

While it might be generally desirable that a child is raised by its natural parents, united in marriage, there are innumerable circumstances which could count against this arrangement in particular cases, and many other reasons why it would be folly to seek to enforce it. Over these reasons and circumstances, the legislation of an inalienable, in the sense of an absolute, right to be brought up by one's biological parents would ride roughshod. Thus, as in the case of the claim for a right to life, it is clear that, if there is such a right, and even if it is inalienable, it would be senseless to take that to mean that it is absolute.[4]

Other, more widely shared, objections to heterologous artificial fertilisation are cited in the document, such as its invasion of the exclusiveness of the conjugal relationship between spouses, the possibility of the child suffering identity confusion, and its general potential to cause damage to the personal relationships within the family. Not mentioned in the section of text where these objections are raised, but obviously also applicable, are the moral objections to *homologous* artificial fertilisation. The primary objection here is that the procedures which are involved break the 'inseparable connection . . . between the two meanings of the conjugal act: the unitive meaning and the procreative meaning' (ch. II, sect. 4, p. 26).[5]

Significantly, this latter statement is extracted from the encyclical letter of Pope Paul VI, *Humanae Vitae*; the pronouncement which, in 1968, finally dashed the hopes of Catholics who thought that the Church might see its way to allowing the moral legitimacy of the use of the contraceptive pill. The objection to homologous artificial fertilisation is the converse of the objection to artificial contraception: the latter involves union excluding procreation, the former involves procreation without union. As it is put in the *Instruction*:

Contraception deliberately deprives the conjugal act of its openness to procreation and in this way brings about a voluntary dissociation of the ends of marriage. Homologous artificial fertilisation, in seeking a procreation which is not the fruit of a specific act of conjugal union, objectively effects an analogous separation between the goods and the meanings of marriage.

(ch. II, sect. 4, p. 27)

On this ground, *in vitro* fertilisation (IVF) in general is deemed morally illicit, along with artificial insemination with donor sperm. Further, homologous artificial insemination is accepted as licit only under stringent conditions, viz., only if it serves to facilitate the conjugal act and is not a substitute therefor, or if it does not involve a dissociation of the unitive and procreative meanings of this act. The last point means, for example, that the obtaining of the sperm by masturbation, even for the purposes of homologous artificial fertilisation, is not permissible.

Despite the insistence on the moral weight of these principles, *no specific injunctions addressed to the civil authorities are based upon them.* The general call to regulate the civil law according to the fundamental norms of the institution of the family, although it might be construed as calling for legal backing for these principles, is in this document clearly given a more restricted application: specifically, it is taken to require the prohibition of gamete donation, embryo banks, *post mortem* insemination and surrogate motherhood. These are to be prohibited primarily because they violate the right ascribed to the child to be 'conceived, brought into the world and brought up by his parents'.

So far as *homologous* artificial fertilisation is concerned, a clear demand for legislation is made upon the civil authority only in view of the manner in which IVF commonly involves the violation of the other inalienable right upon which the document focuses: the right to life and physical integrity from conception:

The law cannot tolerate – indeed it must explicitly forbid – that human beings, even at the embryonic stage, should be treated as objects of experimentation, be mutilated or destroyed with the excuse that they are superfluous or incapable of development.

(ch. III, p. 36f)

The voluntary destruction of human embryos, it is argued, is too frequently associated with IVF, and this occurs in a 'dynamic of violence and domination' which is described as an extension of 'the abortion mentality' (ch. II, prologue; p. 21f).

EMBRYOS, HUMAN BEINGS, AND PERSONS

Recognition of the key inalienable rights is incumbent upon the State because, it is argued, 'they pertain to human nature and are *inherent in the person* by virtue of the creative act from which *the person* took his or her origin' (ch. III, p. 36 – my italics). In other words, *the essence of the document's case for its demands on public policy regarding treatment of the embryo rests squarely on the view that the embryo is a person, or is to be treated as a person, from the moment of conception*, and that this implies that it has the rights which are due to persons. But, if civil authorities are to be expected to heed the appeals of the *Instruction*, then, given that there is no prevailing consensus on the moral status of the embryo, such authorities are entitled to expect a convincing defence of the document's view; one which will stand independently of religious conviction.

Further, although it is common, both inside and outside the Catholic Church, to speak of, for example, the right to life, as a right of *human beings*, in both moral and legal terms it is more accurate to speak of it as a right of *persons*. If 'human being' is understood in a purely biological sense, that is, if to be a human being is simply to be an individual of the species *Homo sapiens*, then it is not apparent why human beings should have any special moral status. It is because human beings *typically are persons*, that special moral status, and arising from that, special legal status, are accorded to them. But, both in moral theory and in law, it has not been universally accepted that *every* human being is a person, or is to be treated *as* a person. Where the dividing line between persons and non-persons is to be drawn, will be dictated by the criteria for personhood. Again, if the view in the *Instruction*, viz., that *all* human beings are persons, is to be pressed on legislatures, it must be argued for in a manner which does not rely upon religious presuppositions.[6]

In Chapter 4, therefore, the nature of Catholic moral reasoning, with particular reference to the establishment of the claims regarding the moral status of human beings as persons, is investigated. The conclusion drawn is that, ultimately, the Catholic teaching rests upon a dogma of faith, viz., that the special status of human beings is a consequence of having been chosen for a unique and privileged relationship *with God, by God.* Thus, knowledge of this status appears to be attainable only through an authoritative interpretation of divine revelation.

However, Church teaching does not generally accept that the case rests on revelation alone. Arguments based on science and philosophy have been deployed to show that the view is also defensible on a non-religious basis, and therefore incumbent on non-Catholics too. Chapter 5 is primarily devoted to an evaluation of the particular argument presented in the *Instruction* for the view that human embryos must be treated as persons. This argument seeks to show that it is implausible to deny that the human embryo, from the moment of conception, is a person. However, it places on some scientific data rather more weight than those data appear able to bear, and also overlooks problematic consequences which would follow, especially within the Church's own traditional and distinctive philosophical-cum-theological perspective.

It has been pointed out that a Vatican Instruction 'simply repeats major principles from recent tradition, and it does not try to refute criticisms raised against them'.[7] It could be argued, therefore, that it is unfair to expect too much of this document: one should look elsewhere for the defence of its decrees. However, a document which makes unambiguous demands on public legislatures cannot, with due propriety, shun the task of defending those demands. Furthermore, the *Instruction* does offer a defence; one which constitutes a summary of the key argument to be found in other documents of the Magisterium and in the writings of those who support the position of the Magisterium (such as Germain Grisez). If there are other lines of defence, then it is incumbent upon the Church to bring them to the attention of those to whom the *Instruction* is directed.

In seeking to show that it would be unreasonable to deny that the embryo is a person, the *Instruction* takes on a more exacting task than the Church has customarily embarked upon. Chapter 6 looks at a less demanding way of defending the status of the embryo. Although this approach is not explicitly adopted in the *Instruction*, it has been a traditional fall-back position in earlier documents and in the writings of Catholic moral theologians, since the latter half of the last century.

In essence, the argument is that, even if there is no proof that the human embryo *is* a person, there is equally no proof that it *is not*, so it *might* be a person. And, if it *might* be a person, we are obliged to treat it *as if it were a person*. But, it will be shown, this argument, if it can be defended at all, can be defended only on a basis which requires a sceptical, dualistic, conception of the human person (i.e., that we can never know with certainty that another individual is not a person, because a person is a composite of two entities, material body and immaterial soul, and the absence of the latter is in principle beyond demonstrative proof). Such a conception of the person is not merely philosophically problematic and, for that reason, unfashionable in the contemporary world. It is quite out of place in the distinctive tradition of Catholic thought identified in Chapter 2, which firmly rejects both scepticism and dualism. And, in any case, it could not serve as a workable basis for the concept of a person in law, where there has to be a way of settling cases in dispute.

CONCLUSIONS

The concluding chapter deals with the implications of these observations for the legitimacy of the Catholic Church calling for legislation to protect the human embryo as if it were a person. It is recognised that there are some persuasive, non-theological grounds for according the legal status of persons only to human beings; that is, grounds for excluding non-human animals. But that does not entail that *all* human beings must be so treated, much less that the circle must include the embryo, which, although undoubtedly *human*, is not undoubtedly *a human being*. The view that all human beings (and human embryos, if they are not human beings) have the rights of persons, particularly the right to life, has not been given a secure foundation which does not rely on theological doctrine.

From a philosophical point of view, argument is, at best, limited to presenting a case for treating the human fetus as a person from the time of the development of the brain activity associated with the activation of the capacities for sensation and motion. This can be defended both from a 'secular' perspective which focuses upon the basis of personal identity, and also from a traditional Catholic perspective applied to current data on embryology.

Finally, it is asked whether, in the face of this inadequacy in the Church's case for embryo legislation, it is legitimate that the case should continue to be pressed. The answer suggested is that it is not, unless, that is, the Church is prepared to abandon principles which have been dear to it (in theory, if not always in practice) throughout past centuries; principles developed by Saint Thomas Aquinas in the Middle Ages, and which marked the sharpest disagreements between Catholicism and Protestantism; principles which would have human society governed by the light of shared reason, rather than by the blindness of one group's dogmatic faith.

2 Mediation and Saint Thomas Aquinas

An understanding of some of the views of Thomas Aquinas is essential in order to come to an appreciation of the current stance of the Catholic Church on questions concerning *in vitro* fertilisation, embryo research, and ethical issues in general, and their perceived implications for civil legislation. This arises first because of the status of Thomas in 'the mind of the Church'; secondly because the salvation-through-mediation theme (enlarged upon in what follows), which was nurtured by, if not rooted in, Thomas' Christianising of Aristotelianism, has been adopted by the Church as its own; and thirdly, because Catholic moral philosophy has become natural law moral philosophy, that is, the prevailing approach to moral issues is characteristically Thomistic, and the Thomistic approach is claimed to be universally applicable.

Further, an understanding of Thomas' views, and the contrast with the other principal pole of the Christian tradition, Lutheran-based Protestantism, will be assisted by a brief consideration of some of the pivotal notions of the ancient Greek philosophers, Plato and Aristotle. In the conflicting approaches to human psychology of these two 'pagan' philosophers lies one of the main roots of the division of opinion among Christians concerning the relation between the divine and the natural orders, and, consequently, of a difference of view on the bearing of divine revelation on moral and legal issues.

SALVATION THROUGH MEDIATION

Let us begin with the salvation-through-mediation theme, the most distinctive hallmark of Catholic thinking within the Christian tradition. By 'salvation-through-mediation' I mean the notion that, except in the most extraordinary circumstances, God's will and grace are believed to be conveyed or channelled to us through some *natural medium*, rather than directly, or by

11

supernatural channels. It is essential to have a grasp of the sources and of the significance of this emphasis in order to assess the teachings and arguments considered later in this book.

The paradigmatic instance of mediation is the divine incarnation in Jesus Christ, which is itself presented to us through the medium of the scriptures. Of course, all Christians, by definition, accept the doctrine of the incarnation, but not all accept the Catholic interpretation that it signifies and confirms the essential goodness of human nature. This interpretation is seen as further reinforced by Christ's appointment of the apostles and their successors as his mediators, a role which is understood to be fulfilled by the pope and the bishops ever since (although it ought to be added that their authority is not held to be directly comparable with that of the scriptures or of Christ; rather they are *interpreters* of the message which has already been given through these primary media).

But mediation does not stop there. The benefit of the incarnation, the grace by which the faithful Christian is saved, is mediated through human agency and the sacramental use of natural materials: water in baptism, oil and laying on of hands in confirmation, bread and wine in the eucharist, and even the forgiving of sins is mediated through the priest in confession. Prayer is regularly directed through Mary, hailed as the Mediatrix, and the various saints. Further, both to underline the key role of the saints as mediators, and in recognition of the holiness of the body, their physical relics are treated with the deepest veneration.

But also, God is thought to operate and to be revealed, not only through these select human agents and sacramental materials, but through nature in general: the existence of God is said to be evident in the natural order of creation and the divine will is believed to be expressed in that natural order. The discerning of God's revelation in nature can be achieved through the exercise of unaided human reason, whereas the revelation given through specific human agents has to be accepted on faith alone, except in a limited domain wherein its content can also be apprehended through reason (we shall be returning to this last point later).

There is a sharp contrast between this approach and that which formed the fundamental thrust of Reformation Protestant thinking, and is currently most in evidence in 'austere' Protestantism of the kind which has been advocated and fostered by, for example, Karl Barth. Here the notion of a medium, whether human or of a more general natural kind, between the believer and God is regarded, at best, with the utmost suspicion. Reformation thought was imbued with a tendency to regard nature, particularly sin-pervaded human nature, as evil and obstructive to salvation. This divergence of views has deep roots which have their origins outside the religious tradition and pre-dating the Christian era. The ultimate source lies in the contrasting theories of knowledge and of human psychology of Plato and Aristotle.

Plato regarded the individual person as essentially a soul which, during this life, merely happens to be temporarily conjoined with a body. This conjunction emerges as a handicap in the pursuit of genuine knowledge and of the Good (that in which our ultimate fulfilment is to be found); bodily passions and impressions continually incline us to mistake the fleeting and the particular (i.e. temporary phenomena) for the enduring and the universal (eternal reality). Nothing worth knowing, in Plato's view, is knowable through the bodily senses for these have access only to the temporal order; knowledge of that which endures can be attained only by that which is itself capable of enduring, viz., the incorruptible soul. Such knowledge is attained through immediate (i.e. non-mediated) recollection of, or direct acquaintance with, eternal reality. Saint Augustine is credited with having 'Christianised' this Platonic view, substituting divine inspiration for Plato's notion of recollection. In doing so, Augustine planted one of the seeds of the Protestant Reformation.

Plato's basic training was as a mathematician, that is, as one who dealt with abstract realities and timeless truths. This undoubtedly played a part in his locating 'genuine reality' with the eternal. Aristotle, by contrast, came from a background in medicine and biology, and, from this empirical perspective, he was led to very different conclusions on these matters. He accepted that there were eternal realities, but also temporal realities. Further, he accepted that the former 'transcended' the latter; they were, in some sense, higher order realities. But he pointed out that this did not mean that only the eternal was genuinely real. The eternal realities for Aristotle were the species, or natural kinds (although particular frogs die every day, this kind of animal, the species, survives).[1] However, for any particular species to exist there have to be particular, temporal, individuals of that species. Thus the eternal reality (the species) is not independent of the reality of the temporal; if the temporal had no reality, the eternal would have no reality either.

What, then, of the individual soul? Must it have a temporal existence only, eternal survival belonging to the human species only as a species? The precise details of Aristotle's views on the immortality of the individual soul are a matter of dispute which will probably never be resolved because of the ambiguity in what remains of his writings, and, in any case, it is not in itself a matter of significance here. What is significant, and is undisputed, is that for Aristotle the individual person is not essentially a soul, but a union of soul and body. Moreover, this union is not a merely contingent conjunction; that is, these are not two separate entities which happen to be temporarily conjoined. The body requires the soul for its animation, as in Plato, but also *the soul requires the body, both in order to have an individual identity and in order to be operative.* Most pertinently for the present discussion, the body is required for the acquisition of *knowledge.* This is because, just as eternal realities have their reality only in the particular, so also they can be known only through the particular, and knowledge of the particular, that is, of concrete individuals, can be gained only through the bodily senses.

Thus, whereas for Plato the soul, or intellect, could have immediate (in the sense of non-mediated) acquaintance with eternal reality, for Aristotle this knowledge has to be mediated through temporal truth and reality, that is, through the temporal process of sensation, whose objects are themselves temporal. Saint Thomas Aquinas did for (or, *with*) Aristotle what Saint Augustine had done for Plato, i.e., arranged an accommodation between the philosophical system and Christian belief. However, Thomas had the stiffer task in that he was faced with a tradition in Aristotelian commentary, mainly of Islamic origins, which inclined to attribute to Aristotle a number of views clearly in conflict with Christian doctrine – for example, that the world is eternal, and that there is no immortality as an individual.

Thomas achieved the marriage of Aristotelianism and Christianity chiefly by going back to the earliest available texts and disputing the interpretations of the Islamic commentators, and, further, by clearly demarcating the spheres of competence of theology, on the one hand, and of philosophy and the natural sciences on the other. For the latter, Thomas maintained, we have to follow the Aristotelian path, and aspire to knowledge of the eternal by attending to sense-knowledge and applying natural reason. In this way much can be learnt, not only enduring scientific truths of an empirical nature, but also such truths as that there exists an Uncaused Cause, that the soul of the human person is immortal, and that stealing is wrong. Truths of the latter kind, in addition to being accessible to natural reason, are also made known by revelation.

There are, moreover, he held, some truths which cannot be attained by our unaided natural powers of reasoning and therefore can come to our knowledge *only* through divine revelation. These include the incarnation of God in Jesus Christ, and certain aspects of God's nature such as its trinitarian composition. But these truths too are *mediated* to us through the particular; through certain historical persons and events. They are not, however, conveyed to us by those events in the manner in which scientific truths can be conveyed by events. For one thing, the events are usually ones which we cannot witness, having occurred centuries ago, and for another, the correct interpretation of the events is not always apparent. Hence *faith*, or acceptance on authority, is required here – both faith in the historical account of the event (i.e., in scripture) and in the interpretation of it (i.e., in Church authority).

This approach of Thomas Aquinas – the 'Thomistic' approach – clearly requires considerable confidence in human nature. We have to accept not only the human authors of scripture as being divinely inspired, but also that the Church, an institution consisting of humans, has divine authority on matters of faith and morals, and that natural human reasoning can attain knowledge both of theological and of moral truths. Luther, by contrast, was prepared to accept only the divine inspiration of the authors of scripture. The authority of the Church to add to, or even just interpret, the divinely-inspired writings was forcefully rejected. Human reason fared even worse, collecting the 'accolade' of 'devil's whore'. Aristotle, he described as 'that buffoon who has misled the Church'.[2] Luther's ground for taking so negative a view was his conviction of the sinfulness of the human race: human nature had become so depraved by sin that nothing human could be trusted. Here we have, in theological garb, the Platonic objections to attending to the senses and their objects: the temporal order can serve only to obscure from us the eternal.

Not all of the reformers were as pessimistic about human nature as Luther. Calvin, for example, could not accept that sinfulness had entirely annihilated the image of God in man (this was his ground for the injunction that every person, whether elected or damned, must be treated with respect), but he still thought that we had to depend on revelation for knowledge, for instance, of the moral law, and for guidance on civil legislation. Although there were differences of emphasis and tone, the distrust of mediated truth, with the exception of that which was mediated through the unadulterated scriptures, was a common and significant theme amongst the reformers.

The Catholic reaction was a staunch defence of Church authority, of natural theology, and of natural law ethics, with Thomas elevated to a previously unparalleled role, even for one sufficiently esteemed to have been made a Doctor of the Church. At the most momentous counter-reformation event, the Council of Trent in 1563, we are told, an altar in the centre of the council chamber bore the sacred scriptures, papal decrees, and the *Summa Theologiae* of Saint Thomas,[3] forcefully symbolising how the man's work had come to be regarded as a reference point for Catholic orthodoxy.

However, it is worth remembering that, despite the central place which has for so long now been accorded to Thomas in Church thought, his views were not always so well received in the Catholic milieu. Indeed only just after his death (in 1274) no less than twenty propositions attributed to him received official condemnation from the Bishop of Paris, and remained condemned for close on fifty years (from 1277 until 1324). The Archbishop of Canterbury, too, although a fellow member of the Dominican Order of friars (the 'Blackfriars') to which Thomas belonged, added his authority to the 1277 condemnations. The following years were marked by controversy concerning the Thomistic Aristotelianism, with the Dominicans eventually rallying solidly behind their prodigy, and the Augustinians and Augustinian-inclined Franciscans issuing further censures on Thomas' teaching and proscribing the reading of the *Summa Theologiae* in their institutions. It was not until after 1323, the year in which Thomas was canonised, that matters began to simmer down, and it was only at the time of the Council of

Trent, when circumstances forced a closing of Catholic ranks, that his dominance became assured.

BODY AND SOUL

Thomas would have been greatly pained by this controversy concerning his teachings, for he never regarded himself as opposing Augustine's views. But it is difficult to be simultaneously both a whole-hearted Augustinian, given that Augustine was a Neo-Platonist, and an Aristotelian. Thomas is often credited with having synthesised Neo-Platonism and Aristotelianism. Although it cannot be denied that his approach was eclectic, eclecticism is not synthesis, and his Augustinian opposition perceived this. A central area of conflict concerned the nature of the union of body and soul, and, as this will be of particular relevance at a later stage, it will be fruitful to explore it in a little detail here.

For Plato, as already noted, a person is essentially her or his soul, and one's fulfilment consists in escaping from the illusions and distractions of embodied life by transcending these through absorption in knowledge of the eternal. Augustine's own experience of life, from his early self-confessed indulgence in debauchery, through his introduction to Neo-Platonism, and his eventual total conversion both to Neo-Platonism and to Christianity, was itself remarkably suggestive of the Platonic model of the course of the soul's escape from the deceitful lures of the temporal world to its state of unshackled bliss in contemplation of the divine. For Augustine, it is as if the soul is entrapped in the body, and the body is not only a handicap in the Platonic sense (i.e., in being a temporal appendage subject to temporal influences), but also in virtue of its being vitiated by sin. Salvation consists in triumphing over the bodily passions by becoming acquainted with eternal truth, which is to be found in the mind of God. But, because we are enmeshed in sinfulness, this can be achieved only by divine intervention: if we are saved, it is by divine predestination alone, and our salvation consists in being freed from the shackles of corporeality.

The attitude of Thomas to the body was much more positive than this, and sprang from his Aristotelianism. If the soul is the essence of the human person and is by nature separable from the body, as Plato, and Augustine following him, claimed, then there could be no individual immortality, as all persons share one essence (one's essence, in this sense, being that which makes one a member of a particular species). Aristotle had not, clearly at least, argued for the immortality of the individual soul, but he had argued against the separate existence of essences in general – this was a fundamental point in his opposition to Platonism. As has been seen, if essences exist, in Aristotle's view, they exist only by virtue of the existence of individuals. And if there are many individuals with a common essence, then the essence can be individually instantiated only if it includes a reference to something which is a basis for differentiating one individual from another.

For example, consider mint one-pound coins. These share *a common essence* in their design or structure or form *and* in their being fashioned from the same physical material. *The individual essence* of a particular coin shares in the common essence, but it is individuated by the particular concrete chunk of material out of which it has been fashioned. It is the material element, *the stuff of the body*, which makes possible the reduplication of the design, the multiple instances of the form of the coin. If the essence of the coin were its form alone, then there could not be more than one coin of a particular form.

Now, both for Aristotle and for Thomas, the essence of all substances in the natural, or physical, world consisted in this form–matter composite; a theory which is known as the *hylomorphic* (literally: 'matter–form') theory of substances. Note, as remarked earlier, that the union of matter and form is not a contingent union; the form of a one-pound coin has no real existence except in particular material coins, and no material can exist without *some* form. When applied to the human person the upshot is that we can no longer think of the essence of the person as an immaterial soul in temporary union with a material body. The essence of the person has to be thought of as an *embodied soul*. The embodiment of the soul is natural, that is, the soul is by nature embodied, and without this the human person would not have an individual soul, which is to say that there would not exist an individual human person. Thus the dualistic conception of the body–soul union, to be found in Plato and the Neo-Platonists, is firmly rejected by Thomas.

That which troubled the Christian Neo-Platonists about this

account should be evident. If the soul is by nature embodied, how can it survive the death of the body? Some of the Islamic commentators on Aristotle, with whom Thomas had taken issue, concluded that individual immortality was impossible. The solution proposed by Thomas was clever, although perhaps not as clever as it might have been. He claimed that the apparent difficulty revealed, not the incompatibility of the hylomorphic theory with the Christian doctrine of individual immortality, but rather its superiority over the dualist account; for only on the hylomorphic theory is there a rational argument for *the resurrection of the body*, an integral element in traditional Christian teaching on immortality. On the hylomorphic theory, individual immortality (or at least the fullness thereof) *requires* the continued union of soul and body.

But against this, the opposition pointed out, it is evident that the union is not continuous, for the body dies and decays before our eyes. Thomas' response was less than satisfactory, smacking of *ad hoc* improvisation. He accepted that the soul suffers a temporary separation from the body but contended that this was an unnatural state of affairs, a consequence of our sinfulness (bodily death being one of the penalties for original sin), and that, as nature can be only temporarily frustrated, this state of affairs would inevitably be brought to an end. It might have been more persuasive if he had suggested that entering immortal life is not beginning *indefinitely continuing existence* but rather entering *timeless existence* (he did conceive of God's eternity as timelessness rather than as unending duration). In this way, the problem of how individuality is maintained in the interval during which the soul is separated from the body would not arise. On the other hand, construing immortality as timeless existence raises a host of additional problems (which will not be entered into here).[4]

The hylomorphic conception of the human person has extensive ramifications, both theologically and philosophically. Salvation requires not only the salvation of one's soul, but also of one's body; the latter cannot be discarded as irredeemably sin-tainted. Thus human nature as a whole is sanctified or, at least, is potentially sanctifiable. Hence the singular appropriateness of our salvation through divine incarnation and the continuing channelling of grace through the sacraments which involve the use of corporeal elements associated with physical welfare or well-being (e.g., bread, wine, water). Hylomorphism also entails that there can be no pre-existence of the soul, that is, that it can have no separate existence before being embodied. This notion was to be found in Plato but was rejected by Augustine. However, Augustine's rejection of it was a matter of faith rather than of philosophy, for there is nothing in Neo-Platonism to exclude the pre-existence of the soul.

Additionally, *hylomorphism entails that the human soul cannot be embodied in just any chunk of matter – the material structures and organisation of the body which receives a form must be appropriate to the form which it receives.* For example, the form of a dog cannot be possessed by a plant body, because the latter is incapable of enabling the former to realise its potentialities (to activate self-motion, sense-organs, etc.). This is known as *the principle of proportionality* in hylomorphism and, as will be seen later, it is of considerable interest in the debate concerning the status of the embryo.

KNOWLEDGE OF THE NATURAL LAW

Another significant aspect of Thomism, upon which some remarks have already been passed, is the theory of knowledge. This is closely bound with hylomorphism. Having elevated the body to an essential element in the nature of the human person, it is appropriate, at least, that it should have an essential role in the acquisition of knowledge. And so it has. Thomas made his own the Aristotelian dictum: 'there is nothing in the mind which was not first in the senses'. Thus, coupled with the upward revision of the evaluation of the body there went an effective inversion of the Platonic theory of knowledge: a recognition of the indispensability of the senses and a confidence in their reliability and in the reality of their objects.

This confidence was tempered, of course, by an awareness of our sinfulness and the consequent impairment of our nature. But Thomas considered that this impairment had to be limited, and limited far more than even Calvin would allow, for the manner in which all of us are sinful is by being tainted with the sin of our first parents that is, by original sin. This, in his view, did not make members of subsequent generations sin of themselves; rather it only made them more prone to sin. Thus, we might say, the structure of our human nature had been destabilised, but still remained intact. For Luther, on the contrary, it lay in ruins, and hence his total distrust of human reasoning.

Thomas, therefore, was both anti-dualist and anti-sceptical, and these positions were interrelated. A corollary of the essential union of body and soul is the possibility of attaining genuine knowledge through sense experience. Of course it has to be recognised that the two most noted dualists of the Christian era, viz., Augustine and Descartes, were also anti-sceptics. But their manner of refuting scepticism, which was remarkably similar for both of them, only served to lead them deeper into the mire as the history of philosophy subsequent to Descartes, particularly the episode of British empiricism, has shown.

Now, through sense-knowledge and the application of reason the Thomist anticipates our acquisition of scientific knowledge, that is, the discovery of the content of the particular sciences such as biology, physics, chemistry, and mechanics. Through further application of reason, metaphysical knowledge can also be attained, for instance, knowledge of the hylomorphic constitution of substances and of the existence of first principles such as the Unmoved Mover and a Necessary Being. Finally, knowledge can also be acquired of the principles of ethics, for ethics is based on the natural order of things: the good consists not in transcending or escaping the natural order, but in its perfection. Thus we read:

> St. Thomas' ethical system is a natural science and not part of theology . . . it is based on purely natural principles derived from reason and abstraction, just like mathematics, physics, chemistry, or physiology.[5]

Thomas' reasoning was that, if nature is essentially good (as it must be, being God's creation), then the most basic tendencies in the natural order must be tendencies to the good. He discerned three levels of inclination in the human person which indicated wherein the good for us lay:

1. An inclination shared with all things: the desire for self-preservation. From this we may infer laws pertaining to the preservation of individual life.
2. An inclination shared with all animals: the desire to

procreate and rear offspring (which serves to preserve the species). This implies the duties and rights appropriate to family life.
3. An inclination proper to human persons alone: to reason and act in accordance with rational principles. This obliges us to avoid ignorance and to recognise our social obligations (beyond the family).[6]

The ethical principles arrived at in this way, the principles of natural law, have universal application and are not superseded or in any way opposed by a revealed divine law. On the contrary, as natural law is discovered by right reason, and right reason is a 'participation' in the divine or eternal reason, then natural law is a participation in the eternal law, that is, it comprises part, but not the whole, of the eternal law.

But two points of clarification are required here. First, although the natural law is said to have universal application, that is, it is binding on all human beings, this is strictly true only of its most general principles, for example, that we must act in accordance with right reason. The conclusions which may be drawn from these general principles, such as that debts must be paid, are not *universally* binding, but bind only as a general rule, for 'impediments' may arise in particular cases (circumstances which constitute good grounds for not following the general rule). This flexibility in inference from natural law principles has frequently been lost sight of in subsequent expositions, especially in matters relating to sexual ethics.[7] Secondly, although natural law is not superseded by any revelation of the eternal law, nevertheless revealed law is necessary for us because, to begin with, our final end is a supernatural one, and therefore we require divine assistance and guidance to attain it, and next, human judgement is subject to error, as is evident from the disagreements which arise when people rely on their own reasoning.[8]

The revealed law with which Thomas was concerned here was the prescriptive content of the scriptures, whose final interpretation on all matters of faith was the prerogative of the pope.[9] But note that, for Thomas, an object of faith is *something unseen, which concerns the divine*, so that the special competence of the pope does not extend, for example, to matters of natural science, which are proper objects of knowledge and not of faith.

This leaves ethics in an ambiguous position. On the one hand, as seen a little earlier, Thomas portrays it as a natural science, in the sense that it is based on observation of nature. On the other hand, as part of the divine law, acquaintance with it is necessary for salvation and in this way it differs radically from the other natural sciences. Thomas' apparent solution is that for some the conclusions of natural reasoning may be held simply on faith, whereas for others they may be objects of knowledge. This leaves open the possibility of a conflict, not between revealed law and natural law, for that is impossible on his view, but between what is believed to be the revealed law and what is believed to be the natural law. For the sake of unity and confidence, therefore, a final authority on both the revealed and the natural law is required, and this authority is vested in the pope.[10]

THE INFLUENCE OF THOMAS

Three reasons were cited at the beginning of this chapter for devoting some space to an appreciation of the views of Thomas Aquinas: his status in 'the mind of the Church', his contribution to the entrenchment of the salvation-through-mediation theme, and the adoption by the Church of a characteristically Thomistic approach to moral and legal issues. Reference has already been made to the extraordinary status accorded to Thomas by the time of the Council of Trent. But the heyday of Thomism had yet to come. This dawned in the later nineteenth century, starting with the First Vatican Council in 1869 and followed in 1879 with the laudatory encyclical of Pope Leo XIII, *Aeterni Patris*, which called for the works of Saint Thomas to be made the basis of Catholic higher education (effectively, the education of the clergy). Leo XIII claimed, as the special merit of these works, their suitability to the requirements of all ages, and their adaptedness 'to crush those errors which are constantly recurring'.

Even Canon Law, the Church's legal code, was amended, so that Canon 1366 laid down that 'Catholic theology and philosophy be taught according to the method, principles, and doctrine of the Angelic Doctor [viz., Saint Thomas Aquinas]'. At the Catholic University of Louvain, Cardinal Mercier, a totally committed Thomist, founded the *Institut Supérieur de Philosophies* for the promotion of scientific education and research in recognition of the Thomistic/Aristotelian principle that all knowledge begins with empirical knowledge. This was perhaps the most significant concrete fruit of these developments. Mercier, however, is not recorded as being so besotted as another prelate, Cardinal Billot, who suggested that: 'It is Peter from whom Aquinas holds this unique authority',[11] a truly daring claim in a Roman Catholic context with its conception of Peter as the source of *papal* authority.

Adulation of Thomas has abated to some extent in more recent years, but the Second Vatican Council (1962–64) still enjoined that the education of priests be conducted 'under the tutelage of Saint Thomas'.[12] Pope Paul VI, who presided over the later sessions of this Council, expanded on this in an address delivered at the Gregorian University in Rome in 1964:

[St Thomas'] force of genius is so great, his love of truth so sincere, and his wisdom in investigating, illustrating, and collecting the highest truths in a most apt bond of unity so great, that his teaching is a most efficacious instrument not only in safeguarding the foundations of the faith, but also in profitably and surely reaping the fruits of its sane progress.[13]

Let these remarks suffice as an indication of the standing of Thomas in 'the mind of the Church'. Attention has already been drawn to the extent to which the theme of mediation permeates Catholicism, so it remains only to remark on the monopoly of Catholic ethics by the natural law theory. This is but one aspect of the mediation theme: nature is one of the media by which the Divine Will makes itself known. Catholic moral theologians developed Thomas' idea into a vast system of morals in which precepts covering almost every conceivable human situation of moral significance were established and claimed to be based upon natural law. These were incorporated in manuals of moral theology which had to be studied in detail by students aspiring to the priesthood, so that they would know how to assess the sinfulness of those who came to them to confess and ask forgiveness.

The predictable reaction to this unbounded legalism was antilegalism; the rejection of all objective moral order. This emerged in the development of Catholic 'situation ethics' in the late 1940s, but the movement was swiftly condemned by the Church. Another Vatican 'Instruction', issued in 1956, in expressing the errors of situation ethics reveals, at the same time, what is expected of orthodox ethics:

> The authors who follow this system hold that the decisive and ultimate norm of conduct is not objective right order, determined by the law of nature, and known with certainty from that law. . .[14]

Although this instruction effectively killed the anti-natural-law movement within the Church, the episode led to a reappraisal of the manner in which natural law ethics had been allowed to develop. As a consequence of this, and of ecumenical dialogue, moral theologians have tended to reject the detailed legalistic approach of the manuals and have either tried to recover the flexibility of Thomas' original approach or, in some cases, to look for an alternative path by which human reason might secure ethical guidance (i.e., abandoning natural law as Thomas understood it as the medium, but still retaining the fundamental principle that ethics is determinable by human reason).[15] But the teaching authority of the Church does not seem to have seen the necessity for any radical change of approach. Both the encyclical on birth control, *Humanae Vitae*, issued by Pope Paul VI in 1968, and the instruction on embryo research, issued in 1987 by the Congregation for the Doctrine of the Faith, appeal unequivocally to a rigid legalistic conception of natural law.

3 What Price Human Life?

The publication of the document, *Instruction on Respect for Human Life in its Origin and on the Dignity of Procreation*, in February 1987, met with a predictably mixed response. Some, mainly non-Catholics but including some Catholics too, had difficulty in comprehending how an institution which had for so long and so steadfastly swum against the tide of the liberalisation of contraception and abortion, apparently on the ground that procreation constitutes the natural fulfilment of marriage, could now, with equal resolve, oppose the best-intentioned efforts to secure this fulfilment for the significant proportion of married couples who needed the assistance of advanced medical techniques. But, for those who were a little more intimately acquainted with the mind of the Church, the thrust of the *Instruction*'s teaching came as no surprise. Desirable as the *aims* of the procreation technologists might be, the *means* adopted to achieve those aims were perceived to be just as unacceptable as the practices of contraception and abortion, and for closely correlated reasons.

The functions of sexual intercourse, it is argued in Church teaching, are to cement the bond between wife and husband (the 'unitive' function) and to generate new life (the 'procreative' function), and these two functions are concomitant by nature. To endeavour to secure the fulfilment of one function while artificially frustrating or excluding the fulfilment of the other is to violate the natural order; to act contrary to natural law. Contraception does this by pursuing the unitive function while frustrating the procreative function. *In vitro* fertilisation (hereafter IVF) and artificial insemination do so by pursuing the procreative function in artificial isolation from the unitive function.

Additionally, IVF and embryo research typically involve the causing of the death of 'spare' embryos, either by killing them, or by allowing them to die. As the Church's opposition to abortion is based on the teaching that the embryo is to be treated as a person from the moment of conception, then IVF and embryo research are deemed to share in the illicitness of abortion.

DUBIOUS HEADLINES

For those familiar with the principles behind this teaching, it was, therefore, not at all surprising to find the Vatican document heralded by sections of the Catholic press as another display of the resoluteness and consistency of the Church in the face of growing pressures to bend the rules for the sake of desired ends; holding out on the inviolability of natural law, rather than capitulating to the secular criterion of utility. But not all of the more triumphalist expressions of greeting will stand up to careful scrutiny. One, in particular, which will reward some attention was the opening sentence of the editorial in the popular UK Catholic weekly, the *Universe* (13 March 1987): 'The Catholic Church once again stands fast on *the priceless value of a human life*' (my italics).

There can be no doubt that such bold simplicity is journalistically and rhetorically appealing, but it can have no place in the real, concrete world in which moral values have to be assigned, defended, and respected. For example, the most natural interpretation of the claim that human life is priceless is that it may not be taken or sacrificed *in any circumstances*, and further, that it must be preserved whatever the costs, short only, perhaps, of priceless costs. Yet it is patently evident that the Catholic Church has not embraced either of these views. Capital punishment (even for lesser offences than murder), killing in just war, the foreseeable but unintended bringing about of deaths (application of the 'double-effect' principle), the refusal to use 'extraordinary means' to prolong life – all of these, and innumerable comparable practices, have been, and in most cases still are, condoned or even advocated by the Church. None of them, at least on first impressions, seems consistent with the claim that human life must be accorded priceless value.

It is possible that this is too simplistic? Despite the initial appearances, is it possible that all of the aforementioned practices are compatible with assigning pricelessness to human life, so that what has been suggested as the 'most natural interpretation' is in fact a misinterpretation of the claim at issue? To clarify this, it will be useful to consider some of the kinds of cases in which the Church has permitted human life to be taken, or has permitted allowing human life to be lost where this could have been avoided. The least controversial case is probably that of the ascription of the right to kill in self-defence. Indeed, Saint Thomas Aquinas, whose authority in Catholic thought has been noted, argued that we not only have a right to defend ourselves against a potentially fatal attack, but a *duty* to do so, even if that requires killing our assailant. His reason for holding that it was a duty rather than simply a right was that we have a greater moral obligation to care for our own life than for that of another.

DOUBLE-EFFECT AND THE PAULINE PRINCIPLE

But if every human life is priceless, how can we have a *greater* obligation to care for one than for another, even if that one is our own? Perhaps Thomas did not hold the doctrine of the pricelessness of human life. But even if we do not subscribe to the idea of the *duty* of self-defence, but merely to the view that self-defensive killing may be justifiable, difficulties still face us. Precisely how the discussion of Thomas Aquinas on this issue is to be interpreted is a matter of controversy. Some commentators read his account as the first explicit application of the 'double-effect principle', a principle which has played a very significant role in attempts to temper the rigidity of some of the apparent outcomes of absolute moral prohibitions, especially in Catholic moral theory. Recently, philosophical assaults on the principle have resulted in it losing much of its former popularity.[1] Moreover, the soundness of its attribution to Saint Thomas is being questioned.[2] Although Thomas does use the expression 'double-effect' in his discussion of self-defence, it is far from clear that he would subscribe to the principle which was subsequently built around this term, purportedly as an explication of his views. Fortunately, these controversies need not concern us here, but the *moral* genesis of the double-effect principle *is* a relevant matter, and will reward some attention.

The principle is intended to enunciate the conditions under which one might freely *cause* something evil to happen, *foreseeing* that it will happen, and yet not be morally guilty of having *intended* it to happen. Briefly stated, the principle is that, provided

1. that the evil consequence is not that at which one aims, and
2. that it is not a means to achieving whatever it is at which one aims, and

3. that the end at which one does aim is of sufficient positive
   moral value to counterbalance the evilness of the foreseen
   consequence,
then the evil, it is held, is unintended.

If these conditions are satisfied, then the good aim may be
pursued without incurring moral guilt. The principle has been
invoked, for example, to absolve of evil intent the surgeon who
removes the cancerous womb of a pregnant woman in order to
save her life. The resulting death of the fetus, it is argued, is not
the surgeon's aim, nor a means to saving the woman, but rather
a foreseen consequence of the means by which she is saved, viz.,
her hysterectomy.

Whether killing in self-defence can meet the criteria of the
double-effect principle is debatable, as also is the question
whether the Church is committed to holding that it does.
Nevertheless, the Church has consistently acknowledged the
right, if not the obligation, to self-defence. Simultaneously, the
Church has clung to the so-called *Pauline principle*, that is, that
one may not do evil in order to secure or preserve some good.
This principle is based upon remarks made by Saint Paul in the
Epistle to the Romans 3:8 and 6:1f. At 3:8, Paul describes as
slanderers those who have accused Christians of teaching that
one may do evil as a means to good; at 6.1f. he denies that
Christians may sin so that 'grace may abound'.

But the point made in 3:8 is not necessarily the same as the
point made in 6.1f.; *to do evil* is not necessarily the same thing as
to sin. If 'doing evil' is understood as *knowingly causing something
evil to happen*, then one can do evil in this sense without sinning,
provided that the causing of the evil is justifiable: only unjustified
causing of evil is sin, or, in philosophical terms, *moral evil.* Did
Paul, then, mean simply that we could not do evil in the sense
of *sinning* in order to achieve some good; that is, was he just
making the point that sinning, or moral evil cannot be justified?

This is the interpretation which has been put on the Pauline
principle by several moral theologians in recent years.[3] However,
if that is what the principle comes to, it is but a tautology, for
bearing in mind that a sin, or a moral evil, is *by definition
unjustifiable*, all it says is that unjustifiable evil is unjustifiable.
Indeed, that this is what the principle is held to reduce to is
implicitly recognised when Bruno Schüller, for example, argues

that the Pauline principle is plausible *only if it is taken in the sense in which its denial constitutes a formal contradiction.*[4] Only tautologies yield formal contradictions when denied.

Perhaps all that Paul wished to do was to emphasise that sin was sin, but it is implausible to suggest that this is the interpretation of his principle in post-medieval Catholic tradition and current in recent teaching of the Magisterium. Like any tautology, the principle that an unjustifiable evil is unjustifiable is compatible with *any* moral theory, even one which accepts that the end can always justify the means. But it is precisely to combat that kind of reasoning that the Pauline principle is invoked; the underlying notion is that there are some means which are intrinsically evil and can *never* be justified by the circumstances. Pope Paul VI had in mind 'the intrinsic evil of deliberate contraception' when he declared:

> it is never lawful, even for the gravest reasons, to do evil that good may come of it . . . even though the intention is to protect or promote the welfare of an individual, of a family or of society in general.[5]

It is surely disingenuous to suggest that this was intended to be understood as nothing more than a disguised tautology.

Moreover, it would be difficult to understand why the elaborate (and questionable) reasoning of the principle of double-effect should have been devised and so steadfastly defended, if the Pauline principle had been taken as a tautology. The emergence and survival of the principle of double-effect is intelligible only as an attempt to meet some potentially very painful dilemmas which arise for subscribers to the Pauline principle, where the latter is understood as proscribing as absolutely unjustifiable the direct or intended causing of evil as a means to one's end. As seen in the cancerous womb case, it attempts to show how foreseeable evil consequences might be brought about in the pursuit of good ends without evil being *done*, in the sense of being intended. Whether the evil is intended, or a foreseeable consequence, makes all the difference only because it is thought that there are certain evil consequences which can *never* be justifiably intended.

Returning to the issue of killing in self-defence, if this is admissable, therefore, it must be *either* that it is deemed to meet the criteria laid down by the double-effect principle, *or* that it is accepted that in the exceptional circumstances in which self-defensive killing is the only alternative to being killed, the Pauline principle is suspended. Because of the restriction imposed by the Pauline principle, for example, it is taught that it is absolutely forbidden *directly* to kill a fetal baby in order to save its mother's life.

It could hardly be clearer that this ethic stands in stark opposition to the utilitarian or consequentialist view that the end justifies the means, or, more precisely, that actions are to be morally assessed solely by weighing the moral values of the consequences which arise, or might reasonably be expected to arise, from them. From this perspective, *how* those consequences are brought about, that is, what means are utilised in securing them, is in itself morally irrelevant. Such an ethic would allow, therefore, that directly killing a fetal baby may be justifiable in order to save its mother's life (but all of the attendant consequences would have to be taken into account before arriving at a definitive assessment of an action's permissibility).

IRRECONCILABLE COMMITMENTS

For the present, evaluation of the relative merits of the Pauline and the consequentialist approaches may be left aside. Of more immediate concern is the difficulty in seeing what sense there is in speaking of the priceless value of human life, even given an unambiguously anti-consequentialist stance. *If* it is never lawful to do evil in order to secure some good, even when, as Pope Paul VI says, the good is the welfare of an individual, or of a whole family, or even of society in general, then it is apparent that human life *does* have its price, for it follows, on this principle, that human life may be, nay, *must* be, sacrificed if it can be defended only by evil means, and this follows *irrespective of how evil* the means happen to be. If the principle is an absolute one, as declared by Pope Paul VI, then no evil, however trivial, may be done for the sake of any good, however great.

But on this perspective, it is clear that *nothing* which might be secured, enhanced, protected, or promoted as a consequence of our actions, neither happiness, welfare, *nor human life itself*, is vested with priceless value. If pricelessness may be attached to anything, it appears that it must attach either to our actions in themselves (it is what we *do* that counts), or to some characteristic or quality of our actions which is not determined by their consequences (such as our intentions, perhaps).

An illustration might help to bring out this point and to illustrate its implications. Suppose that the Secretary of State for Social Services has to reduce spending on pensions over the next four years in order to save ten million pounds. It may be assumed that these savings are required elsewhere for a very worthy purpose, although one for which the state has no special responsibility, e.g. for long-term relief of naturally caused famine conditions in another sovereign state.

The strategy proposed by the Secretary of State is to freeze pensions at their current cash levels, with the result that their real value will be eroded over the four years as inflation increases the cost of living. It is calculated that this freeze, by itself, will be sufficient for the savings target to be reached. In particular, it is evident from the actuarial calculations that achieving the savings required *does not depend on the pensions' freeze resulting in the reduction of the average life-span of pensioners.* Such a shortening of their life-spans might be a foreseen consequence of the chosen strategy, but it is not intended, neither as an end nor as a means to the end. Thus all the conditions of the principle of double-effect would be satisfied.

Now suppose that, following the formulation, but before the implementation of this policy, the Prime Minister, in view of more pessimistic predictions concerning the famine situation and the unavailability of additional funds from other sources, raised the stakes for the Secretary of State, insisting on savings of *twenty* million pounds from the pensions' fund over the same period. The Secretary of State reviews the initial plan and observes that, although no reduction in life-spans was required for making the ten million in savings which was previously demanded, it is statistically evident that the implementation of the plan *would* have resulted in a fairly significant adverse effect on life-expectancy. Indeed, it is clear that this would be of sufficient dimensions that it could be predicted with confidence that an additional ten million in savings would have resulted from the earlier deaths, and hence earlier termination of pensions, which would have been occasioned. Thus, the initially proposed freeze would have been all that was required to yield the full twenty million now being demanded.

What is the Secretary of State to do, assuming that there is no alternative to finding the money by economising on the pensions fund? Surely, we might think, there could be no good reason for imposing on the pensioners an even *greater* cut in income, and consequently greater hardship and *a higher rate of loss of life*? None of this is required to attain the necessary savings, for, as it has transpired, these are going to accrue as a result of implementing the policy previously formulated.

However, *if* the Secretary of State subscribes to the Pauline principle, doing nothing is precisely what will not be permissible. On the contrary, there would be compelling reason to do what, otherwise, would surely be unthinkable: to double the pensioners' hardships, without intending this to benefit anyone! Further, rather than affording an escape from this unsavoury outcome, the double-effect principle *endorses it*.

To see this, consider the available options. On the one hand, the Secretary of State could just continue with the earlier proposal, that is, for having nothing more harsh than a cash freeze, in the knowledge that the earlier deaths of thousands of pensioners will make it possible to meet the increased savings target. Alternatively, reductions in the values (in cash terms) of pensions could be introduced; reductions to a level at which an additional ten million pounds would be saved *even if*, by some unforeseeable circumstance, *life-spans were to remain constant*.

In the latter instance only, the success of the strategy for meeting the target would not *depend* on any earlier deaths, (although it is evident that it *undoubtedly would lead* to far more deaths than the former – it may be assumed that this is statistically indisputable). But the 'advantage' in this strategy would be that the Secretary of State would not cause those deaths *as a means to securing the end required*. The test for whether foreseen consequences of one's actions are means to one's end is to ask whether securing the end by the chosen route *depends on those consequences resulting*. In this instance, the end will be secured even if no earlier deaths occur. On the reasoning of the double-effect principle, therefore, the deaths are a foreseeable but unintended consequence of the action taken. Consequently, the Secretary of State does not *do* anything evil; that is, he or she does not cause the earlier deaths as a means to benefiting the famine victims. And thus the Pauline principle is respected.

The former course of action, on the other hand, that is,

maintaining just the cash freeze, will result in far fewer deaths, but *achieving the end will depend on those deaths resulting.* If this were the option chosen, then the Secretary of State *would cause those deaths as a means to attaining the good which is sought as the end.* Clearly, to act in this way would be to fail to meet the criteria of the double-effect principle, and this would be because it would constitute a violation of the Pauline principle; evil means would be adopted in order that good might be realised; the earlier deaths of some would be caused in order to benefit others. Moral guilt (and nothing else) can be avoided only by resorting to the otherwise unnecessarily drastic policy of eroding both the real and the cash values of pensions.

In defence of the Secretary of State it might be countered that the Pauline perspective would yield this assessment only if it was clear that the intention was to make the required savings at the expense of lives, come what may. This would imply, for example, that if a charitable foundation stepped in to make good the short-fall in pensions so that no earlier deaths resulted as a consequence of the freeze, the Secretary of State would ensure by some other means that life-spans were shortened sufficiently to secure the reduction sought in pensions spending. If he or she were unwilling to do this, it might be contended, it would become clear that it had never been the intention to cause deaths as a means to the end, but only to benefit from unintended deaths.

But all this would show was that the Secretary of State was not prepared to cause deaths in any way other than by reducing the value of their pensions. A reluctance, in the changed circumstances, to take other means of ensuring earlier deaths, is merely evidence of an unwillingness to recognise (or to admit) the moral implications of the initial strategy. Some ways of intentionally causing death appear to be psychologically less daunting than others, but they are ways of intentionally causing death none the less.

The example is somewhat contrived, but this should not matter. It is evident that cases of this kind *could* arise, even if life is usually much more complex, so that one's choices are not normally so restricted. The force of the example is undiminished by this. It shows that, in definable circumstances, one who holds rigidly to the non-tautological Pauline principle, and who deals with dilemmas by way of the double-effect principle, cannot also claim to treat the value of lives as the decisive factor in moral decision-making. What is crucial in this Pauline/double-effect ethic is not the consequence of the action in terms of lives or deaths, but what one *does*, that is, whether *the intention to do evil* can be ascribed to the agent. Indeed this is so overwhelmingly important, it appears, that thousands of lives may be sacrificed if that is what is required 'to avoid doing evil'.

For many of those who reflect on these matters, this implication is likely to constitute a *reductio ad absurdum* of the ethical principles from which it follows. On the other hand, it must be said that abandoning the Pauline principle for thorough-going consequentialism will also lead to some very counter-intuitive and unsavoury conclusions. However, it is not this debate which is our current concern, but rather the senselessness, which should now be evident, of the claim that the Church can teach *both* the absoluteness of the non-tautological version of the Pauline principle *and* the doctrine that human life has priceless value.

THE PRICE OF HUMAN LIFE

Yet perhaps the journalists can be excused their indulging in rhetoric about pricelessness, for the appearance that this is the teaching of the Church is frequently given by many statements emanating from Vatican authorities. In the *Instruction*, for example, it is stated that: 'From the moment of conception, the life of every human being is to be respected *in an absolute way*. . .' (Introd., sect. 5; p. 11). This statement is supported with a quotation from the Holy See's *Charter of Rights of the Family*: 'Human life must be *absolutely respected and protected* from the moment of conception' (ch. 1, sect. 1; p. 12 – my italics in both quotes).

Although the form of expression is different, the content or import is indistinguishable. To say that human life is priceless, or has absolute value is to say that it must be accorded absolute respect and protection, and *vice versa*. At its most basic, what this demands is that we must not harm human life, and must protect it from harm, and this requirement, being absolute, overrides all other requirements placed upon us.

Nevertheless, these prescriptions cannot be taken to entail that one is placed under an absolute obligation to protect any and every life, the fate of which may have come to lie in one's hands.

There are far too many familiar moral dilemmas in which the agent is going to fail to protect *some* lives *whatever* course of action is chosen, from the case of the doctor faced with a choice between saving the fetal baby or its mother, to the more fantastic cases, such as that of the victim of moral ransom who must either carry out an unjust execution or accept the slaughter of the entire nation.

It will be argued, no doubt, that many of these dilemmas are open to resolution in ways which maintain the principle of absolute respect and protection for human life. The double-effect principle is a frequently employed tool here: provided that the lives one is obliged to sacrifice are not forfeited as a means of protecting the lives of the others, it will be claimed that one does not necessarily fail to show them absolute respect and protection. For example, it may be argued that to refuse to carry out the unjust execution is not to intend any harm to those who will perish as a result and, therefore, is not a failure to respect their right to life: only their executioner is guilty of this. However, it has been shown in the foregoing pensions-cutting example that the credentials of this view as an aid to moral decision-making are under severe strain. It might be more honest to say that there are situations in which one life has to be deliberately sacrificed to save another, and provided that it is only in extreme circumstances of this kind that we are prepared to sacrifice a life deliberately, then we render human life as much respect as we are able. Showing *absolute* respect for each and every life is not always a possibility for us.

In any case, the Church has sanctioned and condoned the taking of human life in less closely circumscribed situations than those which might be argued to meet the criteria of the double-effect principle. Let us turn from the popular rhetoric of 'price-lessness' and 'absolute respect', and focus instead on the considered words of the Jesuit moral theologian, Josef Fuchs:

> the preservation or the taking of life are not, in themselves, an absolute value or an absolute evil, else it would not be permissible in any circumstances to kill, or allow to die – and this is contrary to all tradition. Only a correct assessment of advantage, an assessment of the various values and evils implicit in an action (abstract or concrete) makes it possible to establish an absolute. In practice, moral theology has always

applied this principle, for example to the question of what relevant values justify the killing of a man (e.g. capital punishment).[6]

For some, this might seem to amount to pure consequentialism, but to infer that it does would be to misinterpret Fuchs. In unadulterated consequentialism *no* value attaches to anything but the consequences of actions. Fuchs does not wish to deny value to the act itself, or to the intention, but only to deny that either of these has *absolute* value. The refusal to ascribe absolute value to an act, such as the preservation or taking of human life, is quite consistent with the view that *some* value can be ascribed to this act. And this view, in turn, is consistent with allowing that the consequences of an act, or of failing to perform an act, may be of sufficient gravity to override the value ascribed to the act itself. Thus, in a particular context, taking a human life may be a bad thing in itself, and it may have some bad consequences, but the consequences of not taking that life may be worse than the combined badness involved in taking it. In this evaluation, consequences are not all that matter, but they are taken into account alongside the values of actions, so that the latter are not solely decisive either.

Has traditional Church teaching accepted this kind of moral reasoning, as Fuchs claims, or has it been wedded to the absolutes popularly ascribed to it and apparently claimed in some of its authoritative documents? Consider the example offered by Fuchs, namely capital punishment. A defender of absolute respect and protection for human life, or of the non-tautological Pauline principle, cannot justify capital punishment on grounds of utility ('teleological' grounds); that is, the justification cannot be in terms of some good which will be achieved as a result of executing the punishment (such as the deterrence of further crime or the protection of society by the removal of an individual threat to its security). Such kinds of teleological justifications for capital punishment treat the taking of the life of one individual as a means to securing a benefit for others, and therefore treating that particular life as having, at best, a relative rather than an absolute value.

But it might seem that the institution of capital punishment is compatible with assigning absolute respect or value to human life provided that it is justified, and intended, purely *retributively*.

A retributive justification for punishment is one which is purported to be based solely on considerations of justice: the punishment is inflicted on the punished only because she or he deserves it. For the retributivist, any benefit which results from this may be welcomed, but it must not be the *aim* of the punishment. The classical exponent of the retributive theory, Immanuel Kant, argued that respect for the individual *required* her or his punishment, for not to inflict it would be to fail to acknowledge the rational nature of the person, which is the basis of one's moral dignity.

On a theoretical level it might be arguable that the retributive theory meets the demand for absolute respect for human life, for it requires the taking of the lives only of those who have themselves deserved to lose their lives by violating the respect due to others. But, even if that reasoning is thought to be consistent, a moment's reflection will reveal that retributivism cannot be reliably enforced in the real world in which we have to live and conduct our affairs. Whether an accused is found guilty and subsequently sentenced to capital punishment, for example, is a matter of human judgement, and the best human judgement, even with the most sophisticated legal systems we can devise, is not infallible. To institute a system which provides for capital punishment, therefore, is inevitably to risk taking innocent human lives mistakenly, that is, to risk perpetrating the grossest and utterly irreparable injustice.

This is not to say that individual judges who condemn a person to capital punishment necessarily fail to show absolute respect for human life by doing so. If they are wholly convinced of the guilt of the accused, and assuming that retributive capital punishment is consistent with respecting human life absolutely, and they impose the punishment only for retributive reasons, then they do nothing contrary to this principle. Despite this, it is also clear that the judge and jury may not always come to the right verdict, so that incorrect sentencings to capital punishment are likely to occur wherever the institution operates. Thus, *it is having the institution itself* that offends against the principle of absolute respect for human life, for to have the institution is to risk mistaken executions. Taking such a risk, if it is justifiable at all, can be justified only teleologically. Even if the ultimate aim is a purely retributive one, namely to ensure that the guilty are duly punished, the means required, being necessarily a fallible system, involves taking risks with the lives of the innocent. To accept this is to accept that the unmerited killing of some is to be tolerated in the interests of a further end (such as the administration of justice in the majority of cases).

The double-effect principle might be appealed to here, to get the retributivist out of this difficulty. If, for the sake of argument, it is supposed that this beleaguered principle remains sound, it might be argued, because to have capital punishment is not in itself to *intend* the mistaken executions (despite their predictability), then to have capital punishment (to be one of those responsible for its institution) is not to be morally guilty for those deaths. But this will not do, for it is still the case that one would be *risking* these deaths, and to risk the killing of innocent people is not to give their lives absolute respect. It is to treat them as having a *relative* value only: something else must command the greater respect to justify the risk.

The defence of capital punishment, therefore, must, in one way or another, prescind from according absolute value to human life. But, against this it might be retorted that the abolition of capital punishment, too, would be incompatible with absolute respect for human life. Indeed it has frequently been argued that it is because human life is inviolable that capital punishment is the only fitting end for the murderer; that in this way alone can the absolute respect we accord to human life be clearly expressed. While the internal consistency of this view might be debatable, the retort about the implications of abolition may be granted, that is, it may be conceded that the abolition of capital punishment would be incompatible with demanding absolute respect or value for human life. But from this the converse does not follow, that is, this does not show that the demand for absolute respect requires the retention of capital punishment.

On the contrary, the argument of the preceding paragraphs shows that the institution of capital punishment cannot succeed in meeting this demand. Rather, the conclusion which the retort forces upon us is that the demand being placed upon us is simply unrealistic: *absolute respect for human life is something which we are not in a position to exercise.* (Incidentally, Fuchs does recognise *some* absolute values, namely love and justice. These, he says, 'as such may never be violated'. The significance of the 'as such' is unclear, but one can conceive how it might operate to make the ascription of absoluteness to these values arguably tenable. For example, the retributivist might argue that the risking of the execution of the innocent can be tolerated provided that it is done in the pursuit of justice. However, to accept this one would also have to accept that a mistaken sentence, arrived at following a properly conducted trial, would not constitute an injustice.)

The validity of this argument from the condoning of capital punishment might be contested on the ground that a distinction has to be drawn between the rights of the state over human life and the rights of individuals in this respect.[7] The distinction is held to entail that the obligations which bind individual agents are not equally binding upon the state. The state, for example, can take human life in certain circumstances for the sake of the common welfare, or the common good, whereas no individual 'private citizen' may presume to act in a similar fashion. Examples of circumstances appropriate for such state action are where capital crimes are being dealt with and where the just war criteria are fulfilled. Thus, it might be objected that arguments (such as those foregoing) to show the impossibility of operating a system of capital punishment without violating absolute respect for human life are irrelevant when considering the obligations and values incumbent upon individual persons, for individuals (*as* individuals) are not the agents imposing capital punishment.

Against this objection, two points can be made. First, the insoluble dilemmas which crop up in trying to concede absolute respect to each and every human life occur in situations faced by individuals acting in capacities other than as state representatives. A case already mentioned is that of the surgeon dealing with the woman patient who has a life-threatening pregnancy. The allocation of limited medical resources is another typical everyday example, as is the dilemma of how much of my income or wealth I should give to the starving. Secondly, if the obligations which bind individuals can be overridden by obligations to the state, then it is evident that they cannot be deemed absolute. In such circumstances, what demands the *greater* respect is not any *particular* human life, but the common good, so, *a fortiori*, human life cannot require *absolute* respect. Of course, in an ideal society the common good of the state and the good of each of its members would coincide, but, as the Thomistic political philosopher, Jacques Maritain, observed, we do not have a society of 'pure persons', with the consequence that a tension between these goods is unavoidable.[8]

THE INEVITABLE CONCLUSION

Thus, to claim that human life is of absolute value, so that it demands absolute respect and protection, is to claim that obligations are imposed upon us which, on the one hand, the Church has not traditionally imposed upon its members, and,on the other, do not, in any case, admit of the possibility of fulfilment in our practical circumstances. In the light of this, what is to be made of these claims, especially when they appear in official Church documents? Assuming that the position currently taken by the Church is an internally consistent one, there appear to be only two possible options. Either, it must be assumed, the Church has recently radically altered its long-established positions on a multitude of the gravest moral issues and, in doing so, has come to impose an unrealisable ethic, or it has remained fundamentally steadfast in its views while some of those who claim to speak for it have spoken imprecisely, succumbing to the temptation to indulge in hyperbole.

The Church's claim to divinely guided teaching authority on moral matters implies not only current consistency in its teachings, but consistency over time also. This, therefore, constitutes one reason for rejecting the former interpretation (at least it is clear that it would not be acceptable to the Church itself). The unrealistic nature of the demands it would impose is a further, independent, reason for rejecting this option. Consequently, the second of the options is forced upon us, that is, we are obliged to conclude that what is being offered in these claims about the Church placing priceless value on human life or teaching absolute respect therefor, is not a sound interpretation of the Church's position but rather some misleading hyperbolic prose. As will be seen in the next chapter, there might be specific absolute obligations with respect to human life which can be placed upon us, but to require that human life itself be treated as something of absolute value is to impose a requirement which is too frequently impossible to fulfil.

4 Natural and Divine Values

It has been argued in the preceding chapter that, in traditional and established Church teaching, human life is not treated as having absolute value, and, therefore, is not held to command absolute respect, despite occasional, unguarded claims to the contrary. It remains to determine what respect the Church *does* demand for human life. In the course of this investigation, it will also be opportune to pursue the question of the *basis* on which this demand is imposed.

REVELATION AND KNOWLEDGE OF THE MORAL LAW

For Catholicism, as for Christianity in general and, indeed, for any of the traditional monotheistic religions, moral obligation must surely accord with the will of the Deity. It is, however, all too easy to slip from that statement to 'moral obligation is *determined* by the will of the Deity'; and thus to imply that what is presented to one as the divine will should be followed against all natural inclination and rational argument. Those religious persuasions with their roots based in Judaism have a vivid illustration of the possible tension between religious and rational moral commitment in the account of Abraham's experience in being instructed to sacrifice his son, Isaac:

> After these things God tested Abraham, and said to him, 'Abraham! . . . Take your only son Isaac, whom you love, and go to the land of Moriah, and offer him there as a burnt offering upon one of the mountains of which I shall tell you.' So Abraham rose early in the morning, saddled his ass, and took two of his young men with him, and his own son Isaac. . .
>
> When they came to the place of which God had told him, Abraham built an altar there, and laid the wood in order, and bound Isaac his son, and laid him on the altar, upon the wood. Then Abraham put forth his hand, and took the knife to slay his son. But the angel of the Lord called him. . . 'Do

not lay your hand on the lad or do anything to him; for now
I know that you fear God. . .'

(*Genesis* 22: 1–3, 9–12)

A compelling interpretation of this incident is that, despite the
final intervention of the angel, it is made crystal clear that all
earthly values, all human moral intuition and reason, must be
yielded before knowledge of the will of God.

Perhaps this episode, more than anything else, has been
instrumental in confirming that inclination among some Christians, notably Protestants, to insist that ethical guidance is a
matter for direct divine revelation rather than for the calculations
of human reasoning. Although typical of reformers such as
Luther and Calvin, the view pre-dates the Reformation: it was
taken, for example, by William of Ockham in the fourteenth
century. Since the Reformation, however, it has been one of
central characteristics of conservative Protestantism.

Kierkegaard used the account of Abraham's experience to
castigate the rationalism of nineteenth-century Liberal Protestantism and rationalistic ethics in general. For Kierkegaard, the
absolute is to be found only in our relation to God, not in our
relations to our fellow human beings. Abraham's relation to
Isaac, he writes, 'is reduced to the relative as against the absolute
relation to God. . . The absolute duty can then lead to what
ethics would forbid'.[1]

Thus, on Kierkegaard's account, to treat ethical duties as
absolute is to treat man as God, or, rather, it is to create God in
the image of man. Against this, the Thomistic Catholic argument
has been that, although we must not make God in our own
image, neither must we forget that *we have been made in the image
of God*. Consequently, our reason 'participates' in the Divine
reason and, therefore, no conflict will arise between right reason
and the Divine will. This teaching was affirmed most clearly by
the First Vatican Council (1870):

> Although faith is superior to reason, there can never be true
> dissent between the two: for the same God who reveals
> mysteries and infuses faith, illumines the human mind with
> the light of reason.[2]

In moral matters, the light of faith reveals to us the divine law,
given publicly and authoritatively in the scriptures, while the

light of reason reveals the Natural Law, given in the order of the natural world. The Divine Law confirms the natural law and extends beyond it (in so far as it includes particular precepts which are not deducible from natural order, e.g. in prescribing that the Sabbath be kept holy). But, as the order of the natural world is a product of the divine will, divine law could never conflict with the natural law, for both are expressions of the will of God, in whom, as the Council reminded us, contradiction cannot be found.

Yet this proclaimed bold confidence in human reason has had little material impact. The Church lays claim to divinely given authority to interpret the divine law, and, as this includes the Natural Law, then it reserves to itself the role of final arbiter here too. The position was re-emphasised by Pope Paul VI in the encyclical *Humanae Vitae*:

> No member of the faithful could possibly deny that the Church is competent in her Magisterium to interpret the natural moral law. It is in fact indisputable . . . that Jesus Christ, when he communicated his divine power to Peter and the other apostles and sent them to teach all nations his commandments, constituted them as the authentic guardians and interpreters of the whole moral law, not only, that is, of the law of the gospel but also of the natural law, the reason being that the natural law declares the will of God, and its faithful observance is necessary for men's eternal salvation.   (§4)

None the less, the Church does teach that neither public revelation, nor its own teaching authority is *essential* for the acquisition of knowledge of natural law.

NATURAL LAW AND CIVIL LEGISLATION

This teaching entails that, if a moral prescription is said to be evident from the natural order, then it stands independently of divine revelation. Indeed it is *because* such rules or prescriptions stand independently of revelation and are held to be, in principle, accessible to all who care to apply their reason to the issues, that they are regarded as universally binding. And it is because of this that they are to be respected by civil authorities, irrespective of religious persuasion, when considering legislation and its enforcement. It has long been accepted in Church teaching that civil authorities are not required to take account of the areas of divine law which extend beyond the natural law. The reasoning behind this has been that not all citizens in the civil state will be recipients of divine revelation and, therefore, are not bound by it, and, in any case, the business of civil authorities is to pursue and defend the *common good* of the citizenry, which is adequately catered for by the natural law. This task, moreover, does not require that these authorities must legislate for the *whole* of the natural law, but only for those elements of it which conduce to the common good.

This principle has been recognised by Catholic thought since the time of Augustine in the fourth century. Although Augustine sanctioned the use of coercion against the Donatist heretics in his later years, the justification for this was not that they were theologically wayward, but rather that they were opposed to common civil authority. The general principle was unambiguously re-stated by Saint Thomas Aquinas in the thirteenth century, and will be found in Catholic political comment to the current day. The document with which this work is primarily concerned, the *Instruction* relating to embryo research states:

> The task of the civil law is *to ensure the common good of people* through the recognition of and defence of fundamental rights [i.e., rights based upon 'the natural condition and integral vocation of the human person'] and through the promotion of peace and of public morality. . . *It must sometimes tolerate, for the sake of public order, things which it cannot forbid without a greater evil resulting.*
>
> (chap. III; p. 36 – my italics)

The last sentence makes reference to things which are in themselves against the natural law, but which cannot be proscribed in civil law without undue, or disproportionate, detriment to the common good (it has been argued, for example, that prostitution ought to be condoned – legally, not morally – on this principle).

CHURCH TEACHING AND NATURAL LAW

It will be crucially important, therefore, in order to clarify the implications of the Catholic position on the treatment of human embryos, and on the wider question of the value of life, to determine not only precisely what are the relevant prescriptions intended by the statements of the Magisterium, but also whether these prescriptions are based upon natural law alone, or whether they also require acceptance of the revealed divine law. However, this poses a difficulty, for although a great deal of Church moral teaching has been offered as based upon the natural law, the details of the argument from first principles are seldom worked out. One critical commentator remarks:

> I should like to point out a fact about [Catholic] clerical education which may have something to do with the defects of the argument from nature. In seminaries and clerical universities [where those who exercise the Magisterium receive their education] it seems to be nobody's job to expound the argument. The course in moral philosophy does not include it, and the course in moral theology mentions it only as something presumed to be already familiar.[3]

These remarks were written in a context in which the direct concern was the argument from natural law against contraceptive practices, but the point might be given a general application. In fact, there has been *more* explicit treatment of the argument from natural law in this area, viz., that of sexual practices, than in any other, so if the argument seems defective here it is likely to be found even more inadequate elsewhere. In order to acquire some grasp of the characteristics of natural law argumentation, therefore, it is likely to be most profitable to consider the way in which it has been applied in the area of sexual ethics.

When Pope Paul VI endorsed the Pauline principle ('it is never lawful, even for the gravest reasons, to do evil that good may come of it') in *Humanae Vitae*, the evil which particularly concerned him was the 'intrinsic wrong' of 'sexual intercourse which is deliberately contraceptive'. The alleged intrinsic wrongfulness of this practice was declared to reside in its direct conflict with the natural law:

> The Church, in urging men to the observance of *the precepts of the natural law*, which it interprets by its constant doctrine, teaches as absolutely required that any use whatever of marriage must retain its natural potential to procreate human life.

This particular doctrine . . . is based on the inseparable connection, established by God, which man on his own initiative may not break, between the unitive significance and the procreative significance which are both inherent to the marriage act.

The reason is that the marriage act, *because of its fundamental structure*, while uniting husband and wife in the closest intimacy, actualises their capacity to generate new life, – and this as a result of *laws written into the actual nature of man and of woman.*

(§§11 and 12, my italics)

The basis of the natural law argument here is that the marriage act has a 'fundamental structure' which is inviolate. Any interference with, or departure from, this fundamental structure cannot be justified, even for the most weighty reasons. A point to which we shall return, but which may be noted here in passing, is that this conclusion from the principles of natural law is said to be *absolutely required*. As seen in the first chapter, Thomas Aquinas presented the particular conclusions from natural law as binding only *as a general rule*; exemptions in certain circumstances were conceivable for him.

If the unitive and the procreative functions of our sexual capacities are absolutely inseparable and inviolable in virtue of the fundamental structure of the marriage act, then deliberately contraceptive sexual intercourse, masturbation, sodomy, bestiality, and so on, can all be morally ruled out without any enquiry into the circumstances of their practice. The teaching entails that *nothing* outside of the immediate structure of the acts themselves has any bearing on their morality. In this respect, these prohibitions differ radically from almost all other recognised moral prohibitions. Whether sexual intercourse is contraceptive, or whether an act is an act of masturbation or of sodomy, can be specified in non-moral terms. Nothing more than a descriptive account of the physical structure of the act is required. And the moral judgement, on the natural law argument as presented in *Humanae Vitae*, is wholly implicit in that description (provided only that the act is deliberate).

Thus it is held that these practices, if deliberate, are *always* wrong. But no other practices, in the sense of physical actions, are, simply by virtue of being such actions, held to be always wrong. Although whether, for example, a particular act constitutes an act of *killing* can be specified in non-moral terms, no moral assessment of the action can be deduced from that specification alone. The context in which the act took place, the moral setting of the killing, has to be taken into consideration (even when the act is deliberate).[4]

This feature of the prohibition on killing has been widely accepted by the Church itself, as the examples of self-defence, capital punishment, and just war illustrate. In all of these cases, the moral appraisal of the act of killing is based, not simply on an account of what took place physically, but also involves an assessment of the moral implications of the physical act in its particular context. The teaching of *Humanae Vitae* is that deliberately contraceptive sexual intercourse is immoral *whatever* the context: it is '*absolutely required*' that 'any use whatever of marriage must retain its natural potential to procreate human life'.

It might seem that a comparably context-independent judgement on killing would also be possible if the act were specified in some more detail, for example, it might be laid down that the act is intrinsically wrong if it is the *direct* killing of *innocent* human life. But this fails to secure a parallel, for whether the killing is 'direct' or whether the victim is 'innocent' cannot be determined from the 'fundamental structure' of the act of killing alone; the context of the killing has to be taken into consideration.

The form of natural law argumentation to be found in the moral methodology of *Humanae Vitae*, has come to be known disparagingly as 'physicalism', because it seeks to base moral judgements on physical data alone. It has long been criticised by leading Protestant moral theologians for its disregard of the circumstances in which the act in question took place. Indeed 'physicalism' is now increasingly shunned by Catholic theologians too. As one of the latter, Charles Curran (significantly currently under a cloud of Church disapprobation) has remarked:

> there exists a definite chasm between the way many moral theologians do moral theology and the approach employed in the official teaching of the hierarchical magisterium.[5]

And it is not only those whose orthodoxy is questioned who do not share the approach of the Magisterium. It was seen in the last chapter how Josef Fuchs denies the legitimacy of treating particular actions as always forbidden. The act with which he was concerned there was that of killing, but if his point is valid, it applies equally against holding that, for example, contraception is always wrong and, therefore, always forbidden. But the shortcomings of 'physicalism' are not directly relevant to the question whether there is a basis in natural law for the value attached to human life in Church teaching, for, as has been seen, the Church does not treat the assessment of life and death issues in the 'physicalist' manner. Does this mean that these issues are not determinable by natural law criteria?

NATURAL LAW AND THE SPECIAL VALUE OF HUMAN LIFE

Let us begin again, this time with what has been taken as the first principle of natural law since Thomas Aquinas advanced it, viz., that good is to be done and pursued and evil is to be avoided.[6] From this, given two assumptions, an obligation concerning the preservation of human life may be deduced. The first of these assumptions is that *good is that toward which each thing inclines*, and the second is that *everything tends to preserve itself, according to its nature.* All that Thomas deduces from this is that the Natural Law *pertains* to that by which human life is preserved and death avoided, but it is evident that the manner in which it so pertains is by prescribing the preservation of human life and the avoidance of death.

First, note that the argument, if successful, yields no more than *prima facie* obligation, i.e. an obligation which is binding, all else being equal, but one which may be overridden by conflicting obligations, if these should be more weighty. However, in the light of the discussions in the preceding chapter, no stronger obligation ought to be expected. Secondly, this argument, as so far stated, is no more plausible than analogous arguments which might be produced for canine life, or bovine life, or any other form of life. Thomas acknowledges that the inclination to self-preservation is shared with non-humans, but, if this is granted, then the preservation of their lives too is a good to be pursued (incidentally, it has also been observed that if the Natural Law arguments against interference in the sexual order are sound, then they are equally telling against, for example, sterilisation or artificial insemination of livestock[7]).

One can, of course, reinforce the human case, as against that for the other animals, by pointing to the capacity for greater goods inherent in human life, i.e. that it includes not only the values of conscious or sensitive life, but also transcends these with the value-potential of self-conscious, rational life. Nevertheless, the primitive (in the best sense, i.e. closest to the first principle) natural law argument adduced above implies a *prima facie* case against killing non-human life. This is an aspect of the argument which the Church, despite the claim to be guardian and interpreter of the natural law, has not been at pains to teach and defend. On the contrary, the idea of Albert Schweitzer that *all* life demands reverence receives some sharp criticism from two of the more orthodox and highly influential Catholic moral theologians, John Ford and Gerald Kelly:

> In a word, Dr. Schweitzer's thesis on reverence for life is simply sugar-coated moral poison. He wishes to avoid destroying any life, even the lowest; but he sadly realises that some such destruction is 'necessary'. And when it is 'necessary' it is permitted. The logical conclusion of this supposedly magnificent thesis . . . is that even innocent human life may be directly destroyed when this is 'necessary'.[8]

For Ford and Kelly, and for the Magisterium of the Church, innocent human life is clearly held to be in a category quite apart from all other life. It is assigned a value which is incommensurable with the value of any other form of (natural) life. That which induces Catholic moral theologians and the Church to so estimate the value of human life (and the values held to be inherent in human sexuality) does not appear to be anything implicit in the natural order itself. Before that conclusion is asserted, however, it is necessary to attend to an argument in the work of Saint Thomas, which is sometimes claimed to demonstrate the unique status of human life, i.e. an argument which is held to establish that status conclusively on the basis of reasoning from the natural order alone.

The argument is disarmingly simple: however much knowledge a person may acquire, there remains the natural desire for a more perfect knowledge. Natural desires cannot exist in vain. (This is another application of the Aristotelian principle encountered in the second chapter: nature may be temporarily frustrated, but will always eventually triumph. There it was being employed by Thomas to argue for the resurrection of the body.) It follows, therefore, that perfect knowledge must be ultimately attainable. But the perfection of knowledge consists in knowledge of *the First Cause in its essence*, which in scientific terms would be that which is the explanation of everything else, but in theological terms this state of knowledge constitutes the beatific vision, i.e. direct perception of the divine.[9]

This version of the argument is based on the intellect's pursuit of knowledge. A parallel version is also offered, based on the will's pursuit of good. The significant point of both versions is that it is implied that our *end* (that towards which we incline) lies beyond this finite physical/biological world, for it is clear that the perfections sought are not attainable in this life. And as our end, in the natural law argument, constitutes the fulfilment of our potential for good, then we have a potential for value which transcends all that is solely of the physical/biological order; a potential, the fulfilment of which, is prescribed by natural law. As the argument can apply only to beings with intellect and will, it drives a value gulf between those with these faculties and all other living beings.

Kant attempted to construct moral arguments for the immortality of the soul and the existence of God on a similar line of reasoning.[10] The argument for the immortality of the soul was based on an alleged sense of duty to achieve moral perfection, and the existence of God was argued for on the basis of the duty to bring about the state of perfect justice. The structure of Kant's arguments differs from that of Thomas' in that he deduces the possibility of the fulfilment of these ends by way of a different principle.

Thomas, as has been seen, used the Aristotelian principle that nature always finally triumphs, and therefore a natural inclination must be capable of fulfilment. Kant's move is simpler and less contentious; indeed it is one which seems incontrovertible: *any moral duty is capable of fulfilment*, for anything of which we are incapable cannot be morally obligatory for us. In other words, we cannot be required to do anything which is impossible for us. From this, it follows that, in recognising the duties to achieve moral perfection and to bring about perfect justice (Kant takes it for granted that these *are* our duties, and that the righteous will recognise them as such), we implicitly accept the possibility of the attainment of these ends. But, in doing so, Kant argues, we also implicitly accept the immortality of the soul and the existence of God, respectively, as these are conditions without which these ends would be unattainable. Briefly, the arguments are that moral perfection is unattainable in this life, so there must be an extension to this life in which it will be attainable, and, as no individual creature has the power to ensure perfect justice without the cooperation of an omnipotent, omniscient, benevolent power, God must exist as this power.

One objection which has been levelled at Kant's method of arguing is that it would be more precise to describe the relevant duty, not as a duty to *achieve* moral perfection, or perfect justice, but merely as a duty to *strive* for, or seek, these ends. If this is correct, then the structure of the argument is undermined, because we can strive or seek without achieving or attaining, and immortality, in the one case, and the existence of God, in the other, are required only as conditions of success.

The argument of Thomas is not open to the same kind of objection because of the implausibility of the notion that we desire merely *to seek* perfect knowledge, rather than desiring perfect knowledge, or that we desire to seek the good, rather than the good itself. Despite this relative strength, the argument fails to do what is required here. Kant, for his part, was well aware that he was not presenting a *demonstration* in either argument ('demonstration' is here used in the technical sense of a conclusive proof based upon natural reason). Acceptance of his 'proofs' *required faith*; faith in the possibility of achieving moral perfection, or the attainment of the state of perfect justice. Faith which, simultaneously, implied faith in immortality and in the existence of God. Similarly, Thomas' argument requires faith in the Aristotelian principle on which it rests, that is, in the potential of natural desires for ultimate fulfilment. And again, as the condition of their potentiality for fulfilment is the existence of God (the beatific vision is impossible if God does not exist), then we have no more reason to accept the Aristotelian principle than we have to accept that an omniscient God exists.

In any case, it is not clear that Thomas intended the argument in the way in which some have interpreted it:[11] that is, the suggestion that it was intended as a demonstration might be mistaken. Significantly, Thomas goes on to add that the human intellect is not *naturally* disposed to seek ultimate truth, but has *to be elevated by God to this disposition*. In a perceptive recent contribution to the debate on Thomas' position, Jean Porter remarks:

> Thomas was far too conscious of the qualitative difference between God and his creatures, and moreover too eager to do justice to the inner integrity and completeness of the created realm, to claim that any created process or activity is inherently oriented to a share in God's own proper life.[12]

The implication is that, if we are destined for the beatific vision, then this is not a *natural* destiny, but a *supernatural* one; it is not a destiny built into the natural order *per se*, but rather integral to an order which transcends the natural.

Further, as Porter draws to our attention, the *Summa Theologiae* is scattered with remarks about the natural desire for God on the part of *irrational and even inanimate creatures* (e.g. I, 6.1; I–II, 26.2; 109.3.7). Without being drawn into the question of the consistency of Thomas' various remarks, it can be concluded that (i) having a *natural* desire for God, whatever that may mean, does not distinguish rational beings from others, and (ii), if our proper final destiny transcends the ends possible in the natural order of this world, this is by virtue of a divine superimposition on, or extension of, that earthly order. From this it follows that, in so far as Thomas' argument succeeds in establishing that human life has unique value, it does so only with the aid of a premiss which has to be taken on religious *faith*, and therefore it is not established as a matter of the natural law which is accessible to unaided human reason.

REVELATION AND THE SPECIAL VALUE OF HUMAN LIFE

This conclusion regarding the basis of the Church's evaluation of human life and its treatment receives support in statements made in recent Vatican documents. Consider, first, an extract from the *Instruction* relating to embryo research where the absoluteness of the obligation to respect life is being urged upon us:

From the moment of conception, the life of every human being is to be respected in an absolute way because man is the only creature on earth that God has 'wished for himself' and the spiritual soul of each man is 'immediately created' by God; his whole being bears the image of the Creator. Human life is sacred because from its beginning it involves 'the creative action of God' and it remains forever in a special relationship with the Creator, who is its sole end. God alone is the Lord of life from its beginning until its end: no one can, in any circumstance, claim for himself the right to destroy directly an innocent human being.

(Introd., sect. 5; p. 11)

The statement is effectively a summary of recent Church teaching on the value of life, and its accord with other statements is underlined by no less than seven references in the footnotes to the *Instruction*, including references to four popes and the documents of the Second Vatican Council. Although the statement does not make it expressly clear, it is reasonable to deduce that it implies that the obligation to respect human life in an absolute way is not meant to be taken without qualification. One may presume that, so far as the taking of life is concerned, what it entails is summed up in the final remark: 'No one can, in any circumstance, claim for himself the right to destroy directly an innocent human being'. But this is scarcely sufficient to justify the claim that the Church maintains the *absolute value* of human life: it concedes that one may have a right to destroy *non-innocent* human life, and even innocent human life provided that it is not destroyed '*directly*'. On the other hand, this qualified statement of the obligation with respect to human life promises to be one which can be accommodated alongside the traditionally recognised exceptions to the rule: 'Thou shalt not kill'.

But is the *Instruction*'s statement intended to be understood as an interpretation of natural law, or as an exposition of one of the aspects of divine law which are supplementary to natural law, that is, which can be known only on the basis of divine revelation? Some moral theologians would prefer that this distinction were dropped entirely,[13] but, as we have seen, that would be to depart from a long-established tradition in Catholicism. Additionally, although the wish to blur the distinction may be understandable from a Catholic point of view, others may wish to know, and it is intelligible to ask, whether this teaching has its basis in a religious revelation, or whether it is meant to be evident through rational investigation of the natural order. Indeed, an answer to this question is imperative for the Church itself if it is to hope to prevail upon civil legislatures, especially those composed wholly, or mainly, of non-Catholics.

The case presented in the above passage is manifestly based on religious revelation. It is based first upon the belief that God has made the human being an exception amongst all creatures by wishing this one alone 'for himself'. The expression used in the *Instruction* is taken from the Second Vatican Council's *Pastoral Constitution on the Church in the Modern World*, where the revelation of this wish is said to have been given by Jesus in an act of prayer which 'opened up vistas *closed to human reason*' (§24, my italics). What appears to be implied is that this special selection of the human race is an act of God known only through revelation. The second ground offered for the belief is that the spiritual soul of each one of us is 'immediately created' by God. Reference for this doctrine is made to the encyclical letter of Pope Pius XII, *Humanae Generis*, which concerned the issue of evolution. In this pronouncement, those who would suggest that the spiritual soul is a product of nature are rebuffed: direct supernatural intervention, Pius XII insisted, is required for the arrival of the soul.[14] So this ground, too, requires knowledge which is closed to unaided human reason, being of matters beyond the natural order.

The remainder of the passage continues in like manner; no attempt is made to suggest any ground based upon the natural order itself for the evaluation of human life which is there proclaimed. If conclusive evidence of the Magisterium's position were still demanded, it may be supplied from Paul VI's *Humanae Vitae*:

The question of the birth of children, like every other question which touches human life, is too large to be resolved by limited criteria, such as are provided by biology, psychology, demography or sociology. It is the whole man and the whole complex of his responsibilities that must be considered, *not only what is natural and limited to this earth, but also what is supernatural and eternal.*

(§7, my italics)

Thus, despite the oft-repeated appeals to natural law as the basis for its moral teachings, this law, understood as that which is evident (or can be made evident) through conscientious consideration of the order to be found in nature, and which is accessible to human reason, is admitted to be an insufficient basis for the Catholic evaluation of human life. It is not the human being's place *within* the natural order, but rather her or his *relationship with the divine* which constitutes the only adequate basis for the Catholic view.

Furthermore, arguments such as those of Thomas and Kant, which might be employed to underwrite the ascription of special moral status to human life, not only implicitly beg matters of faith, but, in any case, do not amount to a case for giving *human beings*, as such, any privileged status. In so far as these arguments carry any conviction, they establish a special value for *any being* which has a capacity for knowledge, or for moral perfection. But not all human beings have these capacities, while certain non-human beings might be thought to possess them. Which categories of human beings are excluded is arguable, but clearly the anencephalic (those without significant brain matter) and those with severe, irreversible brain damage would be eliminated.[15] One might also argue for excluding the fetus and very young infants which had not yet commenced cognitive activity, on the grounds that they did not have the relevant capacities yet, but only a potential for acquiring those capacities.[16] On the other hand, some non-human animals have displayed cognitive abilities and apparent moral sensitiveness, such that they have a claim to be *included*. Thus, not even the arguments of Thomas and Kant imply the uncompromising speciesism (discrimination in favour of one animal species) to be found in Church teaching and apparently held to be taught in revelation.

Finally, even granted the imputation of speciesism to God, the proscription on killing which is taken to follow, is heavily qualified. As the *Instruction* reminds us, all that is categorically excluded is the *direct* killing of an *innocent human being*. There are at least four issues of controversy concerning this proscription:

1. How is the distinction between direct and indirect killing to be drawn?
2. Is this a distinction of *moral* significance?
3. What constitutes innocence, in the relevant sense?
4. What constitutes a human being?

The first two questions have received much attention in other moral debates, particularly those concerning therapeutic abortion and passive euthanasia. They have not been of great moment in the embryo legislation debate, presumably because the argument that artificial procreation techniques involve only the indirect killing of embryos has not been seriously contended. The debate has focused, rather, on the question whether that which is killed, either directly or indirectly, is *a human being*.

The question of innocence has not been central either. The relevant sense of innocence in this context would seem to be, not that of *moral* innocence, but simply that of not threatening harm (otherwise, for example, one could not justifiably kill a demented assailant in self-defence). Embryos can hardly be said to be a threat to us (not while *in vitro*, at least), but neither are the majority of non-human beings around us: all these are innocent in the required sense. It is evident that what is taken to make the human embryo special is not its 'innocence', therefore, but that it is *a human being*.

Thus, if it can be shown that it is senseless to describe the embryo as a human being, then not even the theologically based calls for its rights to be respected stand. The next chapter explores this issue, as well as probing further both the theological and moral grounds for giving human beings special status.

5 The Argument of the *Instruction*

In the passage from the *Instruction*, quoted near the end of the preceding chapter, it appears to be taken for granted that it is evident that the human embryo, even in its very earliest stages, is a human being:

> From the moment of conception, the life of every human being is to be respected in an absolute way because man is the only creature on earth that God has 'wished for himself' and the spiritual soul of each man is 'immediately created' by God; his whole being bears the image of the Creator.
>
> (Introd., sect 5; p. 11)

Neither of the reasons given here are reasons for treating the embryo as a human being, but rather reasons for treating human beings with 'absolute respect'. But, even considered as such, the first is weakly supported. The scriptural text on which God's 'wishing of man for himself' is purportedly based is the prayer of Jesus to the Father: 'that all may be one . . . as we are one' (John 17: 21–22). But to assume that 'all' here refers to 'all human beings' seems gratuitous; the prayer is surely open to a variety of interpretations, with the consequence that the text is patently inadequate as a basis for this teaching. Further, the reference to immediate creation of the soul has no necessary implications for the status of the embryo, for the timing of this divine act of immediate (i.e. *non-mediated*) creation has long been a matter of debate, and the Church has never ruled definitively on it, as it occasionally takes pains to point out.

Both this last point, and also that the question is one to which philosophical psychology is relevant, are acknowledged in the *Instruction*'s observation: 'The Magisterium has not expressly committed itself to an affirmation of a philosophical nature . . .' (ch. I, sect. 1; p. 13), i.e., concerning the timing of ensoulment, or the existence of a 'personal presence' (a person is implicitly identified with a human life possessed of a spiritual soul). Despite this acknowledgement, the *Instruction* makes remarks which are

58

tantamount to foreclosing the issue. For example, it is stated that:

> The inviolability of the innocent human being's right to life 'from the moment of conception until death' is a sign and requirement of the very inviolability of the person to whom the Creator has given the gift of life.
>
> (Introd., sect. 4; p. 10)

But how can the inviolability of the person *require* inviolability from the moment of conception unless it is being assumed that there exists a person from that moment?

THE CONCEPT OF A PERSON

It will be advantageous at this stage to try to cast some light on the notion of a 'person'. In the Catholic tradition the term has been widely understood in the sense first given to it by the sixth-century Roman scholar, Boethius: an individual substance of a rational nature. Thomas Aquinas remarks that the *autonomy* of rational beings marks them out specially as individual substances (for 'they are self-movers, and not just as links in a causal chain'), and thus it is befitting that they should have a special name: 'person'.[1] Furthermore, it will be evident, given the nature of his argument (discussed in the last chapter) for our unique position in relation to God and, by implication, for our possession of an immortal soul, that it is only by possession of a rational nature that we may possess an immortal soul (in the argument it is the disposition of faculties of our rational nature, viz., intellect and will, which is taken to imply and demand a supernatural destiny). Unless one had a rational nature it would not make sense to ascribe to one a natural desire for a more perfect knowledge, the condition which requires (according to Thomas) fulfilment in the beatific vision.

Hence, in a theological setting such as in the *Instruction*, 'person' is considered to be inter-substitutable with the notion of a human life possessed of a soul. Some campaigners for animal rights might object to the species-preference implicit in the insistence that the concept 'person' can have application only to *human* life which is capable of rationality, but, as has been seen, this appears ultimately to be held as a dogma of the Christian revelation, and it would be tangential to the issues with which we are currently concerned to pursue the question here.

There is another tendency in the document, however, which it would not be prudent to pass over in this way, viz., the habit of treating 'human life' and 'life of a human being' as synonymous. The Second Vatican Council laid down that 'from the moment of its conception (*human*) *life* must be guarded with the greatest care',[2] and, as already noted, the *Instruction* refers to the statement in the Holy See's *Charter of the Rights of the Family* that '*Human life* must be absolutely respected and protected from the moment of conception.' In the *Instruction* itself, however, the formula, already quoted on two occasions, is: 'From the moment of conception, *the life of every human being* is to be respected in an absolute way. . .' (my italics in all quotes). This is not simply a stylistic variation on the earlier forms of expression. If that is all that the authors intended, then they should have chosen their wording with more care. The wording used implies that there exists *a life of a human being* from the moment of conception, not, as in the other formulations, just something which can be described as *human life*. This is significant because, given the common inclination to equate the notions of 'a human being' and 'a person', an inclination to which this document yields, the formula employed in the *Instruction*, rigidly interpreted, effectively begs the issue of the point of ensoulment.

It is particularly pertinent here to note that the terminology used in the statement of the Second Vatican Council was arrived at only after some heart-searching debate, and the Council's statement was deliberately phrased in this way so that it did not carry implications concerning the question of the timing of ensoulment. Additionally, pressures brought to bear on the commission of the Council responsible for drawing up this text to give a clearer definition of abortion were resisted, with the observation that:

> it is not within the compass of the magisterium of the Church to settle the precise moment after which we are faced with a human being in the full sense. Here we rely on the data of science and on philosophical reflection.[3]

Assuming that 'a human being in the full sense' means a human person, the Council thereby left open the possibility that there might exist human beings which are not persons. The

Instruction, by contrast, treats this idea with incredulity: 'how could a human individual not be a human person?' we are asked in evidently rhetorical fashion (ch. I, sect. 1; p. 13). However, no argument is offered in support of this view. For such a defence we have to turn to the American Catholic philosopher, Germain Grisez. Grisez contends that a person is 'nothing more than a living human individual'.[4] He recognises, of course, that this is a view which is not, and has not been, universally shared, not even in his own Catholic milieu, where Boethius' formulation has traditionally dominated. But, Grisez contends, this definition, like every other one, including his own, is 'equally metaphysical or theological, equally non-demonstrable in terms of analytic reason and empirical evidence'.[5]

In fact Grisez seems to think that where we draw the line between persons and non-persons is almost arbitrary:

> Anyone with sufficient ingenuity in metaphysical argument should be able to construct some sort of plausible theory of personality according to which any one of us will turn out to be a non-person.[6]

Why, then, does Grisez think that his definition should be given preference? Because, he suggests, it is given in *Webster's Dictionary* as the oldest meaning of the word, and because it is a more comprehensive definition than later alternatives, such as 'a being characterised by conscious apprehension, rationality and a moral sense'. Public policy for a pluralistic society ought to accept the more comprehensive view, he argues.[7]

That 'person' was originally used to mean 'an individual human being' is, at best, highly speculative, and almost certainly incorrect. But this scarcely matters. There is a reason for the habitual employment of 'person' as synonymous with 'individual human being', namely that human beings, typically, are characterised by consciousness, rationality and moral sense. This is not true of every human being, of course, so taking all human beings as persons will be a more comprehensive way of drawing the limit than taking only human beings with these characteristics. But, still, this does not mean that this account constitutes *the more comprehensive view* unless it is supposed that *only* human beings can have these characteristics. Again, it must be noted that recent evidence on animal psychology might lead us to doubt this.

In any case, the bare fact that one view is more comprehensive than another is no reason, *per se*, for adopting it. 'An individual animal' is an even more comprehensive definition than that of Grisez, but that does not make it reasonable to adopt it as a definition of a person. There have to be *grounds* for choosing the more inclusive view; grounds for thinking that those individuals excluded by the narrower definition might be being excluded mistakenly. And the grounds for doubt here have to be of more substance than the philosophical sceptic's 'ground', viz., the view that it is *always* possible that we might be mistaken in our beliefs. Otherwise, we should be obliged to treat literally *everything* as if it were a person, for if we did not, it would always be possible that we might be in error.

If the notion 'person' is to be employable at all, then there have to be criteria for personhood, which can be applied in practice. And if the notion is to bear the great moral weight it is usually accorded, then these criteria must pick out characteristics of particular moral significance. Being a member of one biological species rather than of another is simply a non-starter for this role.

Neither is it sufficient to urge, as Norman Ford does, that any philosophical definition must accord with 'the common-sense understanding of ordinary people'.[8] On this basis Ford eliminates what he calls the 'personalist' definition, rooted in Locke's requirement of self-consciousness, because it would exclude infants. Legal definitions are also ruled out on the ground that legislative purposes may require a more restrictive definition than that which embraces 'the natural meaning of the term *person*'. Ford argues that, in ordinary linguistic usage, 'human being' and 'human individual' are interchangeable with 'person', and he effectively proposes that the test of any philosophical definition is whether it preserves this interchangeability.

Ford's definition is that a person is 'a living individual with a truly human nature', or more precisely, 'a distinct living ontological individual with a truly human nature'.[9] An ontological individual is 'a distinct being that is not an aggregate of smaller things, nor merely a part of a greater whole'.[10] An infant is the same ontological individual as the adult into which it grows, and therefore infants are persons despite their inability at that stage of their lives to exercise self-consciousness.

I found it odd that, in support of this contention, Ford has recourse to what is 'universally encoded in civil and criminal law'.[11] He has already indicated that the legal interpretation of 'person' will be disregarded for the purposes of his book, because, as noted above, legislative purposes may lead to restrictions on the 'natural meaning' of the word, that is, certain 'natural persons' may be excluded from the category of legal persons. Could it not also be the case – indeed, *is* it not also the case – that the concept of person is often *extended* in legislation? If so, then we cannot appeal to what legislative practice would *include* in the category of persons, either. In any case, if appeal to legislative practice is to be discounted when it might weigh against our argument, consistency demands that it ought also to be eschewed where it might chance to support it.

Furthermore, these appeals sit uncomfortably alongside Ford's insistence that what is a person is a matter of ontological fact, if this is, as I take it to be, a repudiation of the view that it is a matter of convention, or of value. If there are ontological facts, independent of conventions or values (a matter of philosophical controversy which will not be debated here), could not 'the ordinary reasonable man or woman' be misled about them? Could not 'common understanding' be 'common *mis*understanding'?

In any case, as Ford acknowledges, ordinary linguistic usage can be confusing 'if . . . it is taken to be literally accurate'.[12] He was, at that point, alluding to the use of singular terms to refer to collections; a practice relevant to the use of the term 'embryo' to refer to what Ford would argue is not an ontological individual, but, for example, really a collection of four distinct individuals, held together only by an enveloping membrane (cf. Ford, p. 139: 'We should resist the conceptual and linguistic temptation to attribute an unwarranted ontological unity to an actual multiplicity of developing human blastomeres'). But, if we cannot rely on ordinary linguistic usage in this instance, can we be entitled to appeal to it, as Ford does, in support of the contention that infants are persons, or that 'human being' and 'person' have the same ontological reference?

That being a member of one particular biological species rather than of any other is not itself the significant factor here has been at least implicitly recognised by philosophers since Boethius coined the definition of a person as 'an individual substance of a rational nature': it is having a *rational* nature which matters, not having a *human* nature (in the biological sense). All of the main later accounts, including those of such disparate philosophical traditions as mediaeval scholasticism and British empiricism, are essentially variations upon, or expansions of, Boethius' definition. None features biological criteria, but the interrelated characteristics of rationality, moral agency, and self-consciousness, are almost universal.

Note that it is not here proposed that these criteria ought to be adopted *because* they recur so frequently. Rather, what is being suggested is that they recur so frequently *because they are the morally relevant considerations*. For example, if *x* is self-conscious and *y* is not, then there are reasons for according treatment to *x* which it would not be appropriate to accord to *y*: at the most basic level, *x* can be hurt in ways in which *y* cannot; on a more sophisticated plane, it makes sense to ascribe rights to *x* which it would not make sense to ascribe to *y*, because the rights pertain to interests which only a self-conscious being can have.

There will be occasion to explore the concept of a person in more detail in the next chapter. It will be sufficient for present purposes if it has been made clear that, given its crucial significance in the moral debate, the definition of 'person' cannot be allowed to rest upon either 'ordinary linguistic usage' or 'indemonstrable metaphysics', but must be given an intelligible grounding in terms of capacities which are of moral relevance. If one chooses to take the view of Grisez or Ford, that is, that every 'living human individual', and nothing else, is a person, then, if one's choice is to command the persuasiveness which would *entitle* one to the attention of the civil legislature, it requires a grounding of this kind. That is, a grounding upon which all living human individuals can be shown to differ significantly from all other individuals. If the rhetorical question of the *Instruction*, 'How could a human individual not be a human person?', is to be anything more than a play on prejudice, the issue of the *moral* criteria for personhood cannot be sidestepped.

THE EMBRYO AS PERSON?

In the *Instruction*, however, no cognisance is taken of this. In defence of its claims about the treatment to be accorded to the embryo, the document offers us little more than an argument from genetic determination, drawn largely from the 1974 document on abortion. It will be necessary to quote this passage at length:

> The Congregation recalls the teachings found in the *Declaration on Procured Abortion*: 'From the time that the ovum is fertilised, a new life is begun which is neither that of the father nor of the mother; it is rather the life of a new human being with his own growth. It would never be made human if it were not human already. To this perpetual evidence . . . [here there is *omitted* the text: "perfectly independent of the discussions on the moment of animation", which appeared in the original *Declaration*] modern genetic science brings valuable confirmation. It has demonstrated that, from the first instant, the programme is fixed as to what this living being will be: a man, this individual-man with his characteristic aspects already well determined. . .' This teaching remains valid and is further confirmed, if confirmation were needed, by recent findings of human biological science which recognise that in the zygote resulting from fertilisation the biological identity of a new human individual is already constituted . . . the conclusions of science regarding the human embryo provide a valuable indication for discerning by the use of reason a personal presence at the moment of the first appearance of a human life: how could a human individual not be a human person?
>
> (chap I, sect. 1; p. 13)

The argument may be summarised in four stages as follows:

1. As the life of the fertilised ovum is neither that of the father nor that of the mother, it is a *new* life.
2. This new life is a *human* life, for it could not be made human if it were not human already.
3. This new human life is the life of an *individual*, for its *identity* is established from the first instant.
4. This *new human individual*, which comes into existence at the moment of conception, must surely be a *person*.

This argument faces numerous difficulties, as will become evident in the stage-by-stage critique which follows.

First, while it is undeniable that the life of the fertilised ovum is normally a *new life* in the sense that it is not continuous with any one previous life – in particular, that it is not the life of the father alone, nor that of the mother alone – yet it is in a sense, and in a very important sense to the parents, a life of *both* the father and the mother. If its life derived in no way from theirs, that would radically alter their relationships to it. The sense in which human life is continuous through the generations has been pressed by James Diamond:

> [At fertilisation] human life does not begin. Human life once began, and it is now transmitted in living DNA. Zygotes [fertilised ova] begin, and when they begin they are living. However, the livingness of that which is alive in them antedates the existence of the zygotes.[13]

If the life were new in an absolute sense, then some of the more frequently raised objections to artificial procreation involving gamete donation would be undermined, for the new life would be no more closely related to one set of gametes (those of its parents) than to any other set (thus, for example, gamete donation would not have the potential it now has for creating identity problems for the offspring – or, rather, it would not *add* to identity problems).

What appears to lie behind the emphasis on newness is the attaching of special significance to *genetic discontinuity*. But as Diamond's point reminds us, there is genetic *continuity* too. Further, in order to have a new individual life it is not necessary to have *any* genetic discontinuity. For example, following natural cloning, that is, when identical twinning occurs, at least one individuated new life emerges which may be genetically *wholly* continuous with the life of the earlier embryo (I say 'may be' only to allow for the possibility of the minor genetic mutations, etc., which can occur at any stage in our lives. These aside, an identical twin is genetically continuous with its pre-twinning embryo). Further, as we shall see later, *every* normal human embryo has the potential to produce several individual lives in this manner, that is, without genetic discontinuity.

Does this matter? That depends on how much is made to rest on *genetic identity*. At a later stage (step 3) *everything* hinges on the establishment of an identity which is there 'from the first instant', an identity which is said to be biologically constituted. It is difficult to see what can be intended by this other than *genetic* identity. However, the fact that new individual lives can emerge without genetic discontinuity obliges us to discard genetic identity, at least as a *sufficient* criterion of identity of individual life. Further ramifications of the identity issue will be pursued later.

Turning to the second point: it is hardly deniable that the life of the conceptus or early embryo is *human* life. However, unless other questions are being begged, all that can be intended by this is that it is constituted of living human cells, that is, the force of the remark is purely biological. Yet it is difficult to avoid the impression that something more than biological significance is being invested in 'human' here. The remark that 'It would never be made human if it were not human already' suggests a radical discontinuity between the human and the non-human. But even in the biological (as opposed to the theological – see below) sense of 'human' there is no reason to think that such a radical discontinuity exists, at least as far as the species is concerned. On the contrary, evolutionary theory suggests precisely that the human *did* come from the non-human. It can scarcely be supposed that behind this remark there lies an a priori objection against evolutionary theory, for that would constitute an unprecedented stance on this issue, upon which the Church has consistently remained neutral (in so far as evolutionary theorists did not seek to infer a material basis for the spiritual soul).

The distinction between the human and the non-human has been drawn in other senses, of course, for example, we sometimes mark off the human from the non-human on the basis of psychological or moral capacities, or the distinction may be drawn theologically by assigning (or denying) possession of an immortal soul.[14] It is clear that neither psychological nor moral capacities can be at issue here, for the fertilised ovum has neither a psychological nor a moral life, although if allowed to develop it may eventually grow into a being with both, and in this sense *become human*. As regards the theological sense, the *Declaration on Procured Abortion* makes it clear that its argument is 'perfectly independent' of the issue of the timing of ensoulment, so it leaves open the possibility that an embryo which does not have a soul could come to possess a soul.

The *Instruction* treats the issue with rather more circumspection. As already noted (see text above), in the quotation extracted from the *Declaration* it omits this particular part of the passage. This omission might be thought of no importance but for the remarks which follow: 'Certainly no experimental datum can be in itself sufficient to bring us to the recognition of a spiritual soul', the *Instruction* reads, but *science gives us 'a valuable indication'* (chap. I, sect. 1; p. 13 – my italics). However, as early as step (2) in the argument the claim cannot be that that which does not already possess a soul cannot come to possess a soul, for that would be to beg the conclusion in the most flagrant manner: it would follow inescapably that any embryo which grows into an ensouled human being must be ensouled from the first moment of its existence. In any case, that can hardly be what was intended, because acquisition of a spiritual soul by a pre-existing body has never seemed to constitute a difficulty for theologians or philosophers in the Catholic tradition, from Augustine through Thomas Aquinas to Karl Rahner in our own century. Indeed Rahner suggests that fetal ensoulment and the evolution of a species adapted for ensoulment might be viewed as comparable processes of development:

> In both cases a *not yet human* biological organism develops towards a condition in which the coming into existence of a spiritual soul has its sufficient biological substratum[5] (my italics).

There is, therefore, no reason to think that the life of the early embryo must be human in any stronger sense than the *biological* one, that is, in the sense that the living cells of which it is composed are cells of the kind proper to the species *Homo sapiens*. The judgement that something is human in this sense, is, in itself, a value-neutral judgement, or, at least, it has, by itself, no greater value-import than any judgement that something belongs to any biological species.

The third step in the argument concerns the alleged biological *identity* of the new human life. The establishment of this biological identity is portrayed as the basis for the ascription of individuality to the new human life. But in what does this biological identity consist? That is to say, what does the adult person have in common with the embryo from which it developed, which entitles us to say that these are one and the same individual? Only when this is clear will it be possible to ascertain *in what sense* can they be said to be the same individual.

In the normal case, where nature follows its typical course, adult and embryo will share both spatiotemporal continuity and substantial genetic continuity. But these criteria, even coupled, are inadequate as criteria for sameness of *person*, and some serious difficulties face their being assigned the less demanding role of criteria for sameness of *human being*. Some detail of early embryonic development is required to enlarge on these observations.[16]

Initially, that is, upon fertilisation of the ovum, there comes into existence an individual human cell with a unique genetic combination. This cell then proceeds to self-multiply by division or cleavage. In the cases where adult human life does eventually develop from the initial cell, it is not inevitable that only one such life emerges: two (or more) adults may be both spatio-temporally and (substantially) genetically continuous with the same original cell. In view of the emphasis frequently placed upon genetic uniqueness and identity in debates on the status of the embryo, it is worth noting that, in all cases of embryonic development, continuity of genetic identity is a matter of degree. The *in vitro* fertilisation pioneer, R. G. Edwards, points out that the cells of a Down's syndrome child, for example, are subject to constant genetic modification, and, apparently, this is not something peculiar to such children: the genetic constitution of all of us undergoes at least some fine modification throughout our lives.[17]

Furthermore, if, despite this evidence, the identity of an individual is still held to be grounded essentially in *identity* of genetic coding, then, unless we are prepared to allow that one individual may be sacrificed in order that another may come to exist, gene-therapy of the kind that is currently becoming possible, for example, to eliminate sickle cell anaemia or Lesch–Nyham's disease at the embryonic stage, will have to be deemed morally inadmissable, because it involves modifying the original genetic coding of the embryo's cells, thus destroying the 'genetic identity'. Yet the *Instruction* concurs with the view of Pope John Paul II that the healing of maladies arising from 'chromosomal defects' is permissible, provided no harm is done to 'the integrity' of the life of the embryo (ch. I, sect. 3; p. 16). If its identity is made to reside in genetic identity, can its integrity be maintained through genetic modification?

More intransigent problems arise when spatio-temporal continuity is considered. Up to the eight or sixteen-cell stage in the development of the human embryo, each cell is an independent individual in the sense that once it has been formed it is organically quite independent of the other cells, and, indeed, it could float away from the rest were it not retained in its place by the zona pellucida (the outer membrane of the ovum). After the eight-to-sixteen-cell stage, inter-cellular fusion proceeds to bring this state of affairs to an end. But until such fusion occurs, each cell is not only a free entity, it is also 'totipotential', that is, it is in possession of the full potential to produce a complete fetus, and eventually a baby, given the right environmental conditions. In principle it is possible to extract one of these cells and to place it in an empty zona pellucida, and grow it to term in a womb. This has been done successfully, at least up to the four-cell stage, with the cells of fertilised ova of animals. An essentially similar process occurs, without human agency in the event of natural identical twinning (in this case strictly there is still usually only one zona pellucida, but it forms two chambers).

Moreover, identical twinning is still possible, and does some-times occur, after the sixteen-cell stage. The limiting point seems to be the formation of the 'primitive streak', the distinctly longitudinal cell structure which marks the beginning of the acquisition of human body shape by the cell mass. This occurs shortly after the embryo has freed itself from the zona pellucida and embedded itself in the lining of the womb. This stage, known as the implantation (or in some Church documents, as the nidation) stage typically starts about day seven and is complete by about day fourteen. The primitive streak appears usually on the same day or the day following the completion of implantation. At this point, if the development of identical twins occurs, it takes the form of the emergence of two primitive streaks.

An additional complicating factor is the possibility of the reversal of early identical twinning, that is, two cell-groups which had developed from the original single group (whether artificially or naturally) may recombine, or be recombined into a single group, developing into one fetus. Whether this occurs naturally has been disputed, but there are said to be well-documented cases. Whatever the historical facts here, there is no reason to suppose that it *could not* happen, for, in the first place, it would be difficult to argue that it would be *impossible* for the zonae pellucidae of both embryos to re-unite into a single zona (or for the separate chambers of a zona to merge back into a single chamber), and, secondly, even if that *were* highly unlikely, reunion could still occur at any time from the emergence of the cell groups from their degrading zonae pellucidae (or chambers), that is, from four to five days after fertilisation, until the initial stages of implantation had passed (after day seven or eight).[18]

SOULS AND EMBRYOS

These several phenomena give rise to some acute difficulties for the ascription of identity as an individual human being to the early embryo. These difficulties are further aggravated if it is assumed that to be an individual human being is to be a *person*, where to be a human person is understood to require *possession of an immortal soul*. Yet this is precisely the sense in which the Church has traditionally understood 'human person'. It is implied in the *Instruction*'s own remark: 'By virtue of its substantial union with a spiritual soul, the human body . . . is a constitutive part of the person who manifests and expresses himself through it' (Introd., sect. 3; p. 8).

First, if it is held that the original cell of the fertilised ovum is ensouled, what is supposed to happen when, for example, the embryo splits into twin units (or even into three, four, or more)? It has been suggested that all that this requires is the infusion of additional souls at the point of division of the embryo. But if we suppose that this is what takes place, then, strictly speaking, the second (or subsequent) individual is not the direct offspring of the parents of the original fertilised ovum, but rather a cloned offspring of the individual constituted by this ensouled ovum (the parents would now be grandparents, and there would exist a single-parent family in the womb!). In any case, there are no apparent grounds for declaring one of the emerging twins as primary and the other as secondary, the twinning process being simply a division of the cell-group or mass into sub-groups, each of which is totipotential *before* this division.

This latter observation has suggested to some non-Catholics that the difficulties faced by the Catholic position here could easily be resolved by saying that one human being has become two.[19] Indeed, this same point is made by the substantially Catholic influenced organisation, Life ('Save the Unborn Child'), in its commentary on the Warnock Committee Report on embryology.[20] Having suggested that twinning might not be a difficulty because it could be genetically determined from fertilisation, so that it is only *observed* at a later stage, the commentary continues:

> But suppose twinning does truly occur independently some time after fertilisation. . . What do we conclude? Certainly there are now *two* human beings, *two* individuals, *two* embryonic persons who share the same genetic inheritance. Yes. But before there were two, was there none? Of course not. There was one. *One* somehow became two.[21]

But this begs a host of problems concerning individual, and especially personal identity; problems which are insoluble for Catholicism without the abandonment of the traditional account of the soul as immortal in virtue of its simplicity. That is, the incorruptibility of the soul has been made to rest on the alleged indivisibility of that which is incomposite and unextended. If, as has been suggested, 'split-brain' experiments have shown that human beings are divisible, this would create some problems for the indivisible soul thesis. However, the correct interpretation to be placed on the split-brain evidence is a matter of dispute, so it may be conceivable that it could be reconciled with the indivisibility of the soul.

But if such a soul is postulated for the embryo from the moment of conception, empirical evidence about which there can be little dispute would lead us to some bizarre conclusions. For example, if it is supposed that, in the event of identical twinning, a second soul is created and infused at the 'instant' of division of the cell-group, then what would be held to occur in the event of recombination of the twin groups? Nothing has perished in this eventuality, that is, no human tissue has perished. What, then, has happened to the second soul? It looks as though there has been a death without a body! Apart from any other considerations, this would give rise to theological difficulties in connection with the doctrine of the resurrection of the body.

Further, the occurrence of identical twins has no apparent genetic determinant. Rather, it seems to be the result of causal factors extraneous to the embryonic cells themselves (physical pressures on the zona pellucida, primarily). The fact that identical twinning can be artificially induced reinforces this conclusion. Now, if it is supposed that the original totipotential cell is a unique individual person in the theological sense, that is, such that it would be possessed of a soul, is it also to be supposed that the four-cell embryo is this same unique individual?

Alternatively, is it that each of the four totipotential cells is a unique individual by itself, one of them identical with the original, and three new arrivals? Although each of these cells is genetically identical with the original, and is also biologically independent of the others (any three could be removed and the remaining one would survive to grow into a fetus), it must be doubted that any theologian would wish to contend that they were individually ensouled. If anyone did hold this to be the case, then their contention would have to face a multiple accumulation of the difficulties mentioned in connection with the possible recombination of twins.

On the other hand, if plural ensoulment is not assumed, that is, if it is thought that there still exists only one unique individual, then some puzzling moral-cum-theological conundrums arise. For example, how are we to describe what has been done by the obstetrician who extracts one of the four totipotential cells from an embryo because, let us say, the cell shows (genetic) malformation, and then, leaving the remainder to develop into a normal fetus, discards the extracted cell? On the supposition that each totipotential cell at this stage is *not* an ensouled individual, the obstetrician can be said to have simply removed some diseased tissue for the benefit of the ensouled individual which continues to survive within the zona pellucida. Yet what he destroys probably has no less potential for development into a human person (albeit, possibly a handicapped one) than the original totipotential cell: were it to be given the same protection (restored to a zona pellucida) and nutrition as the other cells, it could grow into a fully-fledged fetus. From this perspective, it is difficult to see the justification for not treating it as having the same status as the original fertilised ovum. Yet, in the natural course of events, it most probably would never have developed into an independent individual.

In the light of these considerations, it is puzzling to find it maintained that:

> the conclusions of science regarding the human embryo provide a valuable indication for discerning by the use of reason a personal presence at the moment of this first appearance of a human life.
>
> (*Instruction*, ch. I, sect. 1; p. 13)

particularly when it is apparent that 'a personal presence' is intended to be understood as the presence of a spiritual soul. If the evidence of science indicates a personal presence at that stage, then the same evidence must be taken to indicate *four* personal presences at the four-cell stage, and the passing away of persons as the potentiality for separate embryonic development is lost. But this is clearly absurd.

The 'scientific evidence' upon which the argument relies so heavily is that the genetic coding of the embryo is *new, unique, and remains constant from the moment of conception*. But, as has been seen, this coding is not necessarily new or unique, and its constancy is a matter of degree. The evidence suggests rather that it is inappropriate, not only to think of the embryo as being possessed of an indivisible soul or a personal identity, but even to think of it simply as an individual human being from the moment of conception. From a scientific perspective, the early embryo presents itself as a dynamic structure of human cells with a wide range of potentialities. For example, it could develop into one or more human beings, or it could just form a troublesome mole or cyst in the womb. At its earliest stages, the embryo cannot properly be said to be the individual human being into which it may come to grow, any more than the clay on the potter's wheel is already a particular pot.

THE POTENTIALITY ARGUMENT

Of course, the clay on the potter's wheel may well be a *potential pot* (if it is of the right quality), and similarly, the embryo may be a potential human being, or a potential person. But potentiality is not actuality and does not confer the rights or the endowments which pertain to actuality. That this principle is implicitly recognised in the thinking of the Magisterium is evident when it is found necessary to emphasise that the early embryo must be regarded as 'not a potential human being but *a human being with potential*'.[22]

But does this view make any more sense than the claim that the clay on the potter's wheel is not a mere potential pot but *an actual pot with potential*? Two features of embryonic development are offered to support the Magisterium's perspective: the establishment of genetic identity at conception, and the 'profound continuity' of the process of development. The shortcomings of genetic identity as a criterion of individual identity have already been addressed. But, even if substantial and unique genetic identity were maintained by a particular embryo, this would not constitute sufficient grounds for deeming it a *person with potential*. Equally, there might be maintained substantial and unique *chemical identity* in the production of a pot from a lump of clay, but that does not lead us to deduce that the lump of clay was a pot before it was fashioned.

It might be objected that a false analogy is being used here, because whereas, on the one hand, the embryo, although it requires certain extrinsic conditions for its development, has a principle of development which is essentially *intrinsic*, the clay on the potter's wheel, by contrast, has *no* intrinsic capacity to fashion itself. The clay's becoming a pot is a process in which the clay is purely passive and *that* is why it is inappropriate to speak of it as *a pot with potential*; it has no intrinsic potential of the kind proper to the embryo.

This objection can be met by substituting other analogies. Consider, for example, the trusty acorn. It makes just as little sense to insist that the acorn is not merely a potential oak tree, but already a real oak tree, although one with much undeveloped potential. Perhaps, then, what is crucial is the second feature of embryonic development to which appeal is made viz., its 'profound continuity'. There is a contrast here between the human embryo and the acorn in that, typically, *the acorn remains dormant until it is planted and germinates*. From the point of germination onwards, it begins to make increasing sense to describe the developing plant as an oak tree with potential. But note that *before germination* the acorn already possessed all of the genetically determining factors which would become operative in its later stages: it was not *fertilisation* that was required for the initiation and subsequent development of its growth, but the right environmental circumstances, followed by *nutrition* (through roots and leaves).

The human embryo is not known to exhibit a similar dormancy stage (although it can, of course, be induced by freezing), but, aside from that, it is arguable that the pre-implantation embryo is analogous to the pre-germination acorn. It does not begin the implantation process before reaching the womb, and before implantation it does not *grow*, as it has no source of nutrition. The multiplication of cells in the pre-implantation stage occurs by successive sub-dividing of the material which constituted the original cell, that is, the fertilised ovum. The growth of the umbilical cord at implantation is analogous to the growth of roots and stem in germination.

Further, in several mammals the pre-implantation embryo (known as the *blastocyst* at its most developed stage) can lie dormant *for months* before implanting itself in the uterus and 'germinating'. Evidence has been cited for the European badger, in which this period can last up to fifteen months, the roe deer, in which it lasts five months, and several other mammals, including seals, mink, and otters.[23] This suggests that, after the manner of the acorn, the blastocyst ought not to be thought of as 'a mammal (of the appropriate kind) with potential' until, at the earliest, implantation has taken place. The fact that this phenomenon is not known to occur in human procreation does not dissipate its relevance. As Diamond observed:

> Now badgers are badgers and humans are humans, but blastocysts are still blastocysts, and there is nothing in the above-cited parallels to weaken the argument that the blastocyst stage of the human gestational process is where an *intervital* form of existence must take implantation into a receptive donor of vital capacity before it 'springs' into life.[24]

In view of this (and other considerations), Diamond suggests that we should identify conception with *implantation*, rather than with *fertilisation*.

CONCLUSION

It has to be concluded, therefore, that no persuasive argument has been presented for deeming the embryo a *person*, or even merely an individual human being, from the moment of conception (understanding 'conception' as traditionally understood, i.e. as fertilisation). On the contrary, closer scutiny of the scientific evidence which is invoked points firmly away from this conclusion and suggests that it would be more appropriate to regard the early embryo as simply a structure of human cells with a range of potentialities for development into one or more individual human beings. But does this evidence amount to a *proof* that the embryo is *not* a human person? If it falls short of that, might it not be held that we ought at least to treat the embryo *as if* it were a human person, for it is still possible that it might be one? It is to this argument, which I have labelled the benefit-of-the-doubt argument, that the discussion now turns.

6 Doubt and Scepticism

The authors of the *Instruction* are concerned to show that it would be unreasonable to deny that the human embryo is a person from the moment of conception. In this, they take upon themselves a heavier burden than that which has generally been assumed by their predecessors, who have contented themselves with the thesis that the embryo *might* be a person. So even if the argument of the *Instruction* is unconvincing, we could still be bound to treat the embryo as a person if this alternative strategy is secure, that is, if we are bound to treat as a person anything which *might* be a person, however improbably. Let us begin by trying to elucidate this argument.

THE BENEFIT-OF-THE-DOUBT ARGUMENT

Suppose that a building were about to be demolished by the use of high explosives. In such circumstances, the demolition team would have a serious moral responsibility to ensure that the building had been cleared of human occupants. If there remained any doubt about this, then, all else being equal, the demolition ought not to go ahead. And if, despite these circumstances, they went ahead and it transpired that a human occupant was killed in the process, the demolishers would certainly be morally guilty of manslaughter (or possibly murder), and probably could be successfully charged therewith.

The principle of the benefit of the doubt, on which, in Catholic moral teaching, human life from the moment of conception is deemed inviolable, bears some analogy with the principle which the demolition team would be expected to adopt in a situation such as that described above. Reasons advanced by scientists or philosophers for selecting any particular set of criteria for determining the timing of the origin of a person (which here means an ensouled human being) are regarded as always no stronger than opinions, yielding conclusions which have probability rather than certainty. Therefore, the argument goes, there will always be *some* doubt about whether the killing of an embryo or a fetus constitutes the killing of a person, so it is gravely forbidden to do so, just as the demolition team have a serious obligation not to proceed if there is any doubt concerning the occupancy of the building. The 1974 *Declaration on Procured Abortion* states that: 'From a moral point of view, this is certain: even if a doubt existed concerning whether the fruit of conception is already a human person, it is objectively a grave sin to risk murder' and it is added in a footnote that: 'it suffices that this presence of the soul be probable (and one can never prove the contrary)' (p. 8 and fn. 19, p. 16).

It is true, of course, that the analogy proposed above has limitations; in particular that there is nothing in the embryo case which might correspond to the exercise, possible in the demolition case, of conducting a post-event investigation to establish whether a human being *has* been killed. Searching through the remains is not going to reveal anything which was not known before. As it cannot be established in this way that a person died in the assault, then it does not follow that one who kills an embryo is guilty of murder (unless there is some other way of establishing it). The worst that can be said of one from *this* perspective is that one acted in wanton disregard of the loss of a possible person's life (other perspectives may also have a bearing on the morality of killing an embryo, e.g. the implications of natural law for interventions in the procreative process, but these have no bearing on the question whether it constituted *murder* or a risk of murder).

Even the imputation of wanton disregard might be a harsh judgement if one had taken great pains to try to ascertain whether there was any reasonable ground for thinking that the life of a person might be at stake here and had come to some certainty on a negative conclusion, and especially if, in these circumstances, one had acted for the sake of other persons' lives. Such a state of affairs might arise, not only in the obvious situation in which a pregnancy threatens the life of the mother, but also where the loss of some IVF embryos might be unavoidable in a process which makes possible the achievement of successful pregnancies which otherwise could not have been obtained. If the Church is arguing that such considerations could *never* outweigh the minutest residual doubt about the ensoulment of the embryo, then we are threatened with total moral paralysis, for it is always logically possible that one might kill another person unwittingly as a result of *any* movement one might make.

To reiterate a point made in the last chapter, for the Church's position to be tenable there have to be grounds for doubt which are of more substance than the sceptic's thesis that it is *always* possible that we might be wrong.

FURTHER CONSIDERATIONS REGARDING THE CONCEPT OF A PERSON

Ascertaining the probability of the life of the embryo being the life of a person would be a relatively easy matter if the definition which Norman Ford calls the 'personalist' definition were adopted. As expressed by the seventeenth-century English philosopher, John Locke, a person is: 'a thinking intelligent being, that has reason and reflection'.[1] Clearly neither an embryo nor a fetus could meet this definition. Yet this is the definition current amongst many moral philosophers, of whom Peter Singer is typical. Working from this definition, or approximations to it, Singer and others argue that there is no philosophical basis for conceding a right to life to either pre-natal human beings or even new born infants.[2] Clearly, if the idea that the prenatal human being might be a person is to have any probability whatsoever, a broader ranging concept of a person must be employed.

As already noted, Catholic thinkers traditionally have relied on the definition of Boethius, who held a person to be 'an individual substance of a rational nature'. It might be suggested that this definition is no less restrictive than that of Locke, for although an embryo might be an individual substance with a *potentially* rational nature, it does not yet possess operative rationality and is, therefore, disqualified from counting as a person.

However, against this it could be replied that the actual possession of operative rationality is not requisite for having a rational nature: it is sufficient that such powers should be proper to one's natural kind. For example, tulip bulbs on the market stall might be said to be objects of a blooming or flowering nature, but they will not realise the potential of that nature unless they are nurtured in an appropriate environment over a sufficiently long period. Nevertheless, biologically they belong to a flowering species and could, therefore, be said to have a flowering nature. In the same vein, Rosalind Hursthouse suggests that we could accord moral status to individuals, not on the basis of their individual characteristics, but as members of a species with those characteristics.[3] In this way, she argues, we could ascribe a right to life (a right specific to persons) to all human beings without incurring the charge of speciesism (unjustly discriminating against other species), provided that we also accepted that 'killing members of any other *species of persons* is wrong'.

If the notion of the possession of a rational nature were modelled on the tulip bulb analogy, then it might be claimed that human life from the moment of conception (and arguably before then) is in possession of a rational nature. Yet even if it were, this does not entail that it meets Boethius' definition of a person, for that also required that that which possesses the rational nature should be an *individual substance*. Further, the Hursthouse notion of *a member of a species* also implies something having individual identity. In the preceding chapter, the difficulties which face the ascription of individuality and identity to pre-implantation human life were seen, and attention was drawn to the particularly acute complications which arise if ensoulment, in the sense of possession of an indivisible, immortal soul, is ascribed. Even if there may develop from that primitive form of human life one or more beings which eventually acquire powers of reason, it does not follow that at the start there was an individual substance of a rational nature, especially if that means having a soul in the traditional sense. And this is so even if the tulip bulb analogy is granted, that is, if it is admitted that the embryo is of a rational nature.

But all of this is beside the point if the most basic principles of the philosophical approach which the Church has long commended (despite never formally endorsing it), the approach of Thomas Aquinas, are not to be overthrown. Thomistic psychology, as already noted, hinges on the theory of hylomorphism, i.e., the theory that the individual human, or indeed any individual of a living natural kind, is a metaphysical composite of matter and form: its corporeal mass, its body, stands to its soul, as matter stands to its form (whereas generally in this work 'soul' has been used in the sense of the immortal soul of a person, in the current context of the discussion of hylomorphism it will be used to designate the form of any living being, i.e. a being's principle of life, or the principle of organisation of the matter such that the matter has life). The soul of a plant is the seat of its vegetative powers, that is, of its ability to absorb nutrition and grow by cell multiplication. The soul of non-rational animals is the principle by which they have not only vegetative powers, but also motive and sensitive powers. Finally, the human soul is the seat, not only of our vegetative, motive, and sensitive powers which we share with the lower orders, but also and particularly of our *rational* powers.

Now, it is contended, it is not of the nature of anything wholly material to be rational, for the intellect, which is the rational faculty of the soul, is necessarily immaterial. For this thesis Thomas depended on Aristotelian arguments, such as that which is capable of apprehending immaterial forms (i.e. capable of understanding the *essences* of beings divorced from the concrete individual beings of which they *are* the essences) must itself be immaterial. Hence, the rational soul cannot be produced by the human parents through their material contributions to procreation. Neither can it be a product of the parents' own souls, for, as seen in the last chapter, the immaterial soul is unextended, indivisible, and simple. Therefore, it is argued, the rational soul can be produced only by direct creation *ex nihilo*, and this is what constitutes the philosophical ground for the doctrine of *the immediate creation of the soul*, a doctrine described as 'of the Catholic faith' by Pope Pius XII,[4] a designation which implies that it is part of the substance of the faith, and not an option which Catholics may choose to accept or reject.

These considerations manifestly undermine the analogy with the tulip bulb. A special intervention by God is required to bestow a rational nature, understood as an immortal soul, on the product of the human procreative union; the developing human organism will not attain ensoulment of itself, even given all the right environmental conditions.

The points adduced in the last chapter indicated the senselessness of conceiving of ensoulment before individual identity is established. Thomistic psychology, however, demands much more than settled individuality. Despite the insistence on the supernatural character of the soul and on its immediate creation, Thomas was concerned not to be understood as implying a dualistic divide between the natural and the supernatural realms. 'Grace perfects nature' is a recurring theme in his writings, and one which has held sway both with his followers and with the Magisterium in general.

This is just another aspect of the mediation theme which was addressed in the second chapter. The soul is not perceived as a separate entity from the body, contingently associated with it. Rather, souls can be individuated *only* by virtue of union with a material body. Further, without the body the soul is a pure potentiality; it is actually nothing. It comes to have actuality only through intellectual activity, for which it depends on the bodily senses. And the body, in turn, relies totally on the soul for the realisation of its potential for perfection.

The details of the arguments for these theses need not concern us: it is the derived consequence which is of significance here. In order for the body to be capable of fulfilling the role thus assigned to it, it must itself have the material dispositions, that is, the necessary physical organs, including brain matter, requisite for taking advantage of the potential which the soul is capable of activating. And this requirement applies not only to the body appropriate for a rational soul, but to all bodies which might be ensouled, such as those of plants and animals too; the material dispositions, or organisational structures of the body must be adapted to the kind of life proper to the species. This is the principle of proportionality to which allusion was made in the opening chapter.

It was from this Thomistic perspective that Cardinal Mercier set out to re-vitalise Catholic philosophy at the University of Louvain towards the end of the last century. In his book, *Aquinas*, F. C. Copleston observes:

> Mercier was profoundly convinced of the validity of Aquinas' view that our knowledge starts with sense-perception and that metaphysical reflection is based upon knowledge of the material world. He interpreted this as implying that systematic philosophy must pre-suppose a knowledge of the sciences, that it must remain in contact with them, and that it must integrate their conclusions into itself.[5]

Mercier's *Institut Supérieur de Philosophies* operated on these principles; independent, non-apologetic research was positively encouraged. And cognisance was taken of the implications of the results of such research. The massive textbook of philosophy which he masterminded and largely wrote himself,[6] is remarkable for its scientific illustrations, including those of biological cells and the processes of cell division. In Thomistic fashion, Mercier brought the data of biology to bear on his philosophical psychology.

Reasoning from the Thomistic conception of the interdependence of soul and body, he rejected the Platonic suggestion that the rational/immortal soul might pre-exist the body. Concluding that it must be united to the body simultaneously with God's creation of it, he raised the question whether this union occurs at the moment of conception. Mercier allows that this might be the case (for reasons which have no basis in Thomistic philosophy). However, he goes on:

> But it is equally possible and much more probable that the soul is created *during the course of embryonic life.* . . The organic development of the body is a gradual process; in proportion to its organisation life first unfolds itself as the result of an organic principle similar to that in plants; next sensibility appears in virtue of an animal form to which the first one has given place; until finally the embryo has attained all the dispositions requisite for its being vivified by a rational soul. . . The course of nature now awaits the intervention of the One who alone can create, and at this point God creates the rational soul infusing it into the body as its substantial form.

Mercier continues:

> Embryology wonderfully corroborates these speculations of the old Scholastics. . . The first phenomena following fertilisation are of the nature of a comparatively simple process of segmentation. At the first development of the fertilised egg the microscope reveals only layers of cells arranged in a regular manner and constituting what are called the germinal laminae. Later, the lineaments of the organs appear and their differentiation becomes apparent. Again, from the standpoint of physiology, vegetative functions – such as the contractions of the heart and circulation of the blood – are first exhibited; then follows motility; and lastly, and only lastly, the signs of sensitive life.
>
> As to *what precise moment* the embryo reaches the degree of organisation required for its being informed by the rational soul, it is of course quite impossible to determine.[7]

The expression 'what precise moment' in the final remark must be understood in the sense of 'what precise moment *from the point of acquisition of sensitive life*, if the remark is to be consistent with the principles of Thomism. Joseph Donceel, an American Thomist, put the point more bluntly in a forthright article published in 1970:

> Hylomorphism cannot admit that the fertilised ovum, the morula, the blastocyst, the early embryo, is animated by an intellectual human soul. . . Even God cannot put a human soul into a rock, a plant, or a lower animal, any more than he can make the contour of a circle square.[8]

Finally, it may be worth observing that this conclusion is not one which was not anticipated by Thomists; it is not a position to which they found themselves unwittingly committed in the light of advances in embryology since the last century. On the contrary, as Cardinal Mercier remarks, advances in knowledge of the process of embryonic development have done no more than broadly confirm the speculations of the medieval scholastics, and of Saint Thomas in particular. In the document which stood alongside the scriptures at the Council of Trent, Thomas writes: 'At first the embryo has a sense-soul only. When the more elaborate soul, at once sensitive and intellective, comes, the first goes, as we shall see in more detail later'.[9] When we come to discuss the significance of the continuity of embryonic development, we shall have occasion to look at the greater detail promised by Thomas here.

It has been argued that Thomas came to this view only because he was mistaken about certain biological facts: his account, it is said, was based on the belief that the sperm, like the seed of a plant, had to die before new life could come into existence.[10] A difficulty is that Thomas' account of generation is complex. While it is by no means clear that he held the view ascribed to him, what he does say is open to interpretation in that way. But while this mistaken biology might have encouraged him in his thesis, Thomas had no need to rely on it. His conclusion was dictated by the theory of hylomorphism coupled with the principle of proportionality. There can be no doubt that he would have had little difficulty in adjusting to the insights of modern biology. Indeed, like contemporary Thomists, he would have found that the new embryology 'wonderfully corroborates' his original views on the stage-by-stage process involved in the development of a human individual.

THE NINETEENTH-CENTURY PERSPECTIVAL CHANGE

As has been noted, however, Mercier does not treat the argument as secure, but allows that ensoulment *might* take place at conception. Later ensoulment is merely 'more probable'. Placing this qualification on the conclusion became commonplace amongst Thomists from the latter half of the nineteenth century, and it enabled them to avoid coming into direct conflict with the teaching of the Church. It is only a little over one hundred years since the Church ceased to draw a distinction between the ensouled and the unensouled embryo/fetus and began to demand that the embryo be treated as a person from the moment of conception. Before then, neither moral theologians in general, nor the Magisterium itself, saw reason to speak of later ensoulment as only a probability. In the early eighteenth century, Saint Alphonsus Liguori, patron saint of moral theology, regarded it as *certain* that the fetus is not ensouled from the moment of conception, but only after it is 'formed' (a term generally understood in Saint Augustine's sense of a body endowed with an active power of sensing). Indeed the Magisterium sometimes took the view that the burden of proof of the status of the embryo lay with those who would *affirm* its ensoulment: for example, a decree of the Holy Office, issued in 1713, *forbade* the baptising of a fetus where there was no reasonable foundation for regarding it as animated by a rational soul.[11]

An explanation which has been offered for the change in the Church's approach traces its origin back to the proclamation of the dogma of the Immaculate Conception in 1854.[12] The proclamation of this dogma, issued by Pope Pius IX, declared that 'the Virgin Mary was, in the first instant of her conception, preserved untouched by any taint of original sin'. As it is only the soul which can be tainted with sin, the implication is that Mary, from the first moment of her conception, was possessed of a soul. Some fifteen years later, the same Pope issued the Bull, *Sedes Apostolica* requiring the removal from the code of Canon Law of the distinction between the ensouled and the unensouled fetus, making all abortion punishable by excommunication. A revised edition of Alphonsus Liguori's work, *Theologia Moralis*, published in 1896, cites the doctrine of the Immaculate Conception as confirmation of 'the more probable opinion' that the soul is infused at the moment of conception.[13] Since then, the Magisterium has constantly taught, not that the fetus *is* ensouled from the moment of conception, but that it is to be *treated as ensouled*. Whether it is ensouled has been regarded as a question of a philosophical nature on which the Church would not pronounce.

Despite this, the conclusion to which the officially favoured philosophical approach, the Thomistic approach, unambiguously points is not accepted. This would be understandable if there were sound doctrinal findings which were incompatible with the Thomistic view. But the formula used in proclaiming the dogma of the Immaculate Conception was more likely the first signal of the changing attitude of the Church rather than a cause of that change. Whichever is the case, the dogma, however doctrinally sound, does not give grounds for rejecting, or even for casting doubt upon, the traditional Thomistic account of ensoulment. If the dogma entails ensoulment from the moment of conception, then it entails it *only in the case of the Virgin Mary*; it does not entail any general rule on the timing of ensoulment.

Some three hundred years before the proclamation of this dogma, the *Catechism of the Council of Trent* had already taught that the body of Christ was ensouled immediately upon conception. But the Catechism did not see any general rule on the timing of ensoulment implied by this. On the contrary, it was portrayed as a specially significant *exception* to the natural order, in which delayed ensoulment is the norm:

> As soon as the Blessed Virgin gave her consent to the Angel's words . . . at once the most holy body of Christ was formed and a rational soul was joined to it. . . Nobody can doubt that *this was something new* and an admirable work of the Holy Spirit, *since, in the natural order, no body can be informed by a human soul except after the prescribed space of time*[14] (my italics).

Since the Immaculate Conception was also a unique event which required special divine intervention, then it too could have been accommodated to the Thomistic account in like manner. That is, it could have been argued that, while it continues to be the case that the natural order generally exhibits the divine moral order, God, as author of nature, always retains the power to modify or bypass nature, and has evidently chosen to do so in these two very exceptional instances.

If this solution seems to demand too much direct divine intervention, or if it seems doctrinally inappropriate to presume such a close parallel between the conceptions of Mary and of Christ, there is an alternative which avoids both of these drawbacks. It could be argued that 'conception' in the statement of the dogma (and generally) is to be understood as the beginning of Mary's existence *as a personal being*. This would leave open the question whether this event coincided with the beginning of existence of the embryo from which she grew (fertilisation of the ovum). This is the approach suggested by Norman Ford who gives a detailed history of the notion of 'conception', illuminating its different senses.[15]

Either way, it cannot be supposed that ensoulment *generally* proceeds without regard to the natural order. If divine intervention in nature were habitual, then the whole of the framework of the Thomistic theory of knowledge (both of the natural and of the divine) would collapse, and sure knowledge could be acquired only by the grace of revelation. The weight Catholicism has put upon mediation would be misplaced; Luther's distrust of natural 'knowledge' and his blind faith in revelation would turn out to be vindicated. Clearly, Catholicism, as it has been identifiable since at least the Reformation, stands or falls with the *basic principles* of Thomism. Yet it is difficult to reconcile the trend of the Church's approach to the question of ensoulment, as it has developed since 1869, with those basic principles.

DOUBT AND SCEPTICISM

It is not being argued here, and indeed it would be folly to argue, that the Church, or for that matter anyone, ought to place absolute faith in any philosophical conclusion or scientific finding. On the other hand, if the paralysis of scepticism is to be avoided, we have to live and act upon the beliefs to which science and philosophy (and, where appropriate, revelation or theology) lead us. There is, however, one traditionally recognised qualification to this rule which might seem to underpin the Church's stance on the embryo. It concerns cases where the factual evidence for a belief is subject to uncertainty. In such cases, the rule is: 'one may never resolve a factual doubt which endangers the life of a human being by using a probabilistic method of reasoning'.[16]

The illustrations of the application of this principle which are usually provided are likely to prove uncontroversial for moral theorists of almost any persuasion. One is that of the deer-hunter who is unsure whether the movement in the bushes is that of a deer or a fellow-hunter. Another, that of a chemist with reason to think that an unidentified bottle on a shelf has been mis-labelled and contains deadly poison. The scarcely controversial conclusions are that the deer-hunter may not shoot in the direction of the movement, and the chemist may not dispense drugs from amongst the suspect bottles.

The examples are similar to the one considered at the beginning of this chapter, in which a building which could contain a human occupant is about to be demolished. There it was suggested that some analogy might seem to obtain between cases of this kind and the treatment of the status of the human embryo in Church teaching; that is, it sometimes seems as if the Magisterium regards the ensoulment of the embryo as a matter of factual doubt on a par with the doubts which inhibit action in these cases. If there is a sustainable analogy here, it would be difficult to resist the benefit-of-the-doubt argument.

It has already been noted that the analogy has limitations, in that, in the case of the embryo, no further investigations of an empirical nature will yield more information than was initially available about whether a person's life is at stake. It has been seen that the relevant evidence which has been obtained, coupled with the principles of Thomistic philosophical psychology, fur-nishes no good reason for thinking that the human embryo, especially in its earliest stages, is a human person. If, despite this, it is still maintained that it *might* be a person, it is necessary to ask in what sense is 'might' being used here, and, in particular, is it being used in a sense which can sustain the analogy with the deer-hunting or demolition examples.

Carol Tauer, who has painstakingly investigated this question, finds the Magisterium, and in particular the *Declaration on Procured Abortion*, inconsistent.[17] The *Declaration* sets out by treating the timing of ensoulment as a factual matter. However, it then goes on to declare that the issue is not open to resolution by biological science because it is properly a philosophical issue. The problem with this is that it immediately places the doubt about whether there is a danger to human life here in a different category from the empirically resolvable *factual* doubt which arises in the other examples. In the latter cases, the issue could have been settled by greater knowledge of the physical state of affairs. In this case, however, the most complete knowledge of the physical state of affairs is held to be insufficient. But, even more problematically, the *Declaration*, despite its insistence that the issue is a philosophical one, goes on to exclude the possibility that even philosophy could ever definitively resolve the matter by showing that the embryo is not ensouled: 'It suffices that this presence of the soul be probable (*and one can never prove the contrary*) in order that the taking of life involve accepting the risk of killing a man . . . already in possession of his soul' (p. 16, n. 19, my italics).

Note first that the claim that 'one can never prove the contrary' of ensoulment being probable cannot be intended in the sense that one can never show that ensoulment is improbable (in Mercier's fashion, for example). Arguments for its improbability are not excluded because, in Catholic moral theology, being probable is compatible with being improbable. The term is used in the statisticians' sense, that is, in the sense which includes the very lowest probabilities, and not in the familiar colloquial manner in which it indicates being more probable than improbable. In the moral theologian's sense, then, it follows that to show that ensoulment is highly improbable is not sufficient to show that it lacks probability. Secondly, there would have been no point in the remark about the philosophical nature of the issue if philosophical reasoning were thought incapable of arriving at a conclusion on the probability of ensoulment at conception. On the other hand, of course, it does not imply that philosophy is capable of *definitively* resolving the issue.

It follows, therefore, that the *Declaration*'s claim does not exclude the possibility that there could be strong philosophical grounds for considering ensoulment at conception highly improbable. But what the claim entails is that *no matter how strong the philosophical argument and however persuasive the biological evidence on which it stands*, there will *always* remain a probability that the wrong conclusion has been arrived at, and therefore that conclusion may not be acted upon. But this is not a reason for restraint in any way analogous to that which operates in cases of factual doubt such as those which face the deer-hunter, the chemist, or the demolishers. In the embryo case alone, among these four cases, it appears that a *radical scepticism* is required: a scepticism which has more far-reaching implications than its advocates seem to recognise.

If we can *never* be sure that the embryo does not have a rational soul, then we can never be confident that the brain-dead patient, that is, the patient who has lost all brain functions, is not still possessed of a soul. If this were the case, then switching off the life-support system would be morally equivalent to early abortion (abortion before brain activity had become evident). Yet the Church has not only allowed the cessation of life support in situations of this kind, but has conceded that determining the criteria for death is not a matter for philosophers or theologians, much less for the Magisterium, but for medical science.[18]

It might also be argued that, if there is always a probability that a life so primitive as that of the early embryo is ensouled, then there must be an even greater probability that many other beings are ensouled. As Tauer remarks:

> If one relies on empirical data which support the possible presence of a rational soul, there is better positive argument available for animals like mature dolphins than there is for human zygotes, morulae, and blastocysts.[19]

Of course, the *Declaration* tells us that we cannot rely on empirical data, even when reinforced by philosophical reasoning. As has been seen earlier (Chapter 3), an unbridgeable gulf between human beings and other animals is taken to be implicit in the data of revelation. Not only enthusiasts for animal rights, but scriptural exegetes too, might be inclined to see in this nothing more than human prejudice in interpreting revelation. For example, one of the points frequently made in support of human supremacy is that God became incarnate as a *human being*. But if this confers on humans an immeasurably higher status than that of any other animal, could there not be (and have there not been) analogous arguments based on God becoming incarnate as a Jewish, white, male? In any case, all this is beside the point if the principle of the mediation of the moral law through the natural order is not to be abandoned.

If we cannot rely on natural reasoning from empirical data, then the connection between the possession of a rational soul and the natural powers of that which possesses it is severed: for all we could know, *any* particular body might or might not be ensouled, depending on the arbitrary (from a scientific or philosophical perspective) will of God. Thus the notion of the integrating natural unity of body and soul, which Thomas Aquinas placed centrally both in his philosophy and in his theology, and which has substantially shaped Catholic thinking since, would now have to be jettisoned and replaced with a dualistic account in which the union is purely contingent. On this account, the Thomistic principle of proportionality would have to be abandoned – a rational soul could be present in a body which did not have even the power of sensation, or indeed merely the powers of nutrition and growth (as noted earlier, the pre-implantation embryo multiplies its cells by rearranging its original material; it does not receive any significant nutrition or grow in size). From a philosophical point of view, ensoulment of *any* living body could not be ruled out.

The Thomistic anti-dualistic approach at least gives ground for distinguishing between beings who possess the potentialities and faculties required for intelligence (the appropriate brain capacities and sensory organs) and all other beings: possession of a rational soul is conceivable only for the former. It is of interest that the perspective on the origin of a person, to which Thomistic reasoning leads, coincides closely with that to which some secular philosophers are now inclined, that is, that a person exists once there is established a continuity of physical organisation within a continuously existing brain which can support continuities of memory and personality.[20]

'THE ONE WHO WILL BE A MAN IS ALREADY ONE'

This secular and Thomistic insistence on the presence of certain physical structures, it may be objected, overlooks the fact that the organism which comes to acquire these structures was determined to do so well in advance. Hence, it could be argued, this justifies the drawing of a significant distinction between a human embryo and any other living entity with a similar level of biological functioning: while neither currently has the requisite physical structures for intellectual life, one will acquire them through a natural dynamism of development which is absent in the other. No one is likely to deny this, or the observation that this means that one of these beings is potentially a person whereas the other is not. But sometimes a stronger conclusion is drawn here: the *Declaration* expresses it with an oft-quoted passage from Tertullian: 'The one who will be a man is already one.'[21] A statement issued by the Archbishops of Great Britain (1980) put the same point thus: 'Each such new life [of the fertilised ovum] is the life not of a potential human being but of a human being with potential.'[22]

It is particularly surprising that Church authorities should now be quoting Tertullian in support of their teaching on this matter. Tertullian was taken to task in his own time (in the second century) for holding the doctrine of 'traducianism', that is, the view that the soul as well as the body is produced from the parents in procreation. This doctrine, of course, entails ensoulment of the embryo from conception, but it has been consistently rejected by the Magisterium in favour of the doctrine of immediate creation, that is, the teaching that each soul is brought into existence by *direct* divine action, and not through natural agency.[23]

Behind the remark that 'the one who will be a man is already one' can hardly be the thesis that that which is a *potential* such-and-such must be an *actual* such-and-such. To take that view would be to abolish the distinction between potentiality and actuality entirely and the archbishops' statement makes it clear that that is not the intention, for it is still recognised that the fertilised ovum has undeveloped potential. Nevertheless, by parity of reasoning it would appear that we should have to hold that an acorn is not a potential oak tree but an oak tree with potential, the seed-corn is not a potential harvest, but a harvest already, and so on.

The archbishops offer two grounds for their problematic view. The first of these is the continuity of genetic coding. The shortcomings of this criterion as a criterion of individual identity were made evident in the last chapter. As further noted there, if it cannot support individual identity, then continuity of genetic coding can scarcely be a successful candidate for establishing personal identity, that is, identity 'as a man', to use Tertullian's idiom.

The second ground offered by the archbishops is the continuity of the development process;

> The development of this potential is normally a process of profound continuity. No-one can point to, say, the fourth week of that process, or the eighth, the twelfth, the twentieth, the twenty-fourth or twenty-eighth, and say 'That is when I began being me'[24]

Why this absence of discontinuity is taken to intimate that the human being is there from conception is not spelt out in the statement, but one may speculate on what is to be read between the lines. The preceding section of the statement implied that the once traditional distinction between the unensouled and the ensouled fetus was based upon a mistaken impression that there was a biological discontinuity at the moment of 'quickening' (the acquisition of self-moving power). Modern science has undermined this, and so another point of discontinuity has to be sought. This is found only in the 'moment of conception'.

But one is forced to wonder why such biological discontinuity seems to be required for the moment of ensoulment if, as the Magisterium repeatedly claims, ensoulment cannot be determined from biological facts. Furthermore, it is arguable that conception is not unique in the chain of genetic development, a view expressed strongly in the scientific jargon of James Diamond:

> But are some zygotes homines *in potentia?* I suggest that there is a multiple, staged potency in effect here. Some zygotes, once fertilisation occurs, are intrinsically capable of being organismalised by a series of right extrinsic things happening to them, if all wrong extrinsic things are prevented from happening. Yet an ovum has the potency for becoming a homo if the right thing (fertilisation) happens to it. I am not comfortable with divisions of a continuum into subcontinua, and the biodynamic continuum leading to you and me is 3 billion years old. . .[25]

But that kind of reasoning fails to convince those who focus on the appearance of the new genetic combination at fertilisation. Here, it seems, despite the point Diamond makes, there is a new beginning. However, this can be conceded without also having to concede that personal identity or ensoulment must be traced back to that point. Secular philosophers, who have no reason to ignore biological or other scientific facts, are not persuaded that the biological data oblige them to trace personal identity back to conception. Perhaps it might be thought that this is because they can think of the emergence of a person as a gradual process: that being a person can be a matter of degree. The traditional Catholic conception of the soul seems to preclude this: either a being has an immortal soul or it has not. This, perhaps, is why it is felt that the ensoulment event requires a physical discontinuity as its correlate.

But the Thomistic account offers an accommodation between the ideas of biologically continuous development and instantaneous ensoulment in the course of that development. What ensoulment requires, for Thomas, is not physical discontinuity but discontinuity of the immaterial form:

> both in the case of men and of other animals, when a more perfect form supervenes this brings about the dissolution of the preceding one. However, it does so in such a way that the second form possesses whatever the first one does and something more into the bargain. And thus in man, as in the other animals, the final substantial form comes about through many comings-into-being and dissolutions . . . the intellective soul is created by God at the completion of man's coming-into-being. This soul is at one and the same time both a sensitive and nutritive life-principle, the preceding forms having been dissolved.[26]

That is, a process which on the physical level is one of continuous development, brings into existence a succession of beings which have only physical continuity with what went before: the new principles of organisation required at the different stages of development imply that we have new kinds of being emerging, not the same being going through successive stages (the oak tree has physical continuity with the acorn from which it grew, but it is not an acorn, just as an acorn is not an oak tree).

The generation of a human being requires initially a principle of cleavage (Thomas, of course, did not postulate this principle, but this was only because of his ignorance of this aspect of embryology), then a principle of nutrition and growth, followed by a principle of sensation and self-motion, and finally a principle of intellection. Thomas did not think that this committed him to the view of some of his contemporaries that the developed animal or person had several forms or souls. Each successive form, in his account, incorporates the functions of the form which preceded it (his main argument for this was that the organisational unity of the animal or person could not otherwise be explained).

Thomas' view, therefore, does not require any biological discontinuity: all it entails is that for ensoulment a certain level of biological development has to be attained, but there is no reason why this cannot be arrived at through a gradual, continuous process. This approach, unlike that of Tertullian, is also eminently adaptable for coming to terms with the theory of evolution (as Karl Rahner appreciated: 'In both cases a not yet human biological organism develops towards a condition in which the coming into existence of a spiritual soul has its sufficient biological substratum'.[27]

Thus we are not obliged to say that what will become a human being or person *is already* a human being or a person. Describing the life of the early embryo as the life 'not of a potential human being but of a human being with potential' is without convincing warrant. The richer the concept of 'human being' that is being employed, the less warrant it has, but as was seen in the last chapter, not even the most impoverished concept, viz., 'biologically human individual', appears applicable. At the other end of the spectrum, if it is the presence of human personhood that is in question, then not only is the postulation of such a presence from the moment of conception untenable, but even the traditional benefit-of-the-doubt argument cannot be invoked to uphold the principle that it should be treated *as if* it were a person; not, at least, if dualistic scepticism is to be avoided.

7 Revelation and Legislation

In an introduction to *The Warnock Report on Human Fertilisation and Embryology*, Mary Warnock writes:

> We were obliged moreover to bear in mind that any law must be generally seen to be beneficial, that it must be intelligible and that it must be enforceable. The law must not outrage the feelings of too many people; but it cannot reflect the feelings of them all. It must be drawn up with a view to the common good, however this notoriously imprecise goal is to be identified.[1]

The Church is in full agreement with the principle that the law must be formulated so as to seek the common good. It also offers some guidance on how that goal might be identified: in the words of the Second Vatican Council:

> the common good embraces the sum of those conditions of social life by which individuals, families, and groups can achieve their own fulfilment in a relatively thorough and ready way.[2]

The Council went on to note that this will require a positive system of law which would 'recognise, honour, and foster' the rights of 'all persons, families, and associations'.[3]

It is accepted, however, that any positive legal system will have inevitable limitations. Hence, although the whole of morality might be said to be oriented toward recognising, honouring, and fostering the rights of all persons, families and associations, Church documents repeatedly acknowledge that civil law cannot be expected to cover the moral sphere in its entirety.[4] In particular, civil law must often tolerate certain evils which could not be prohibited without greater evils ensuing. But this policy of expediency is itself subject to limitation, as the *Declaration on Procured Abortion* reminds us:

> The law is not obliged to sanction everything, but it cannot act contrary to a law which is deeper and more majestic than any human law: the natural law engraved in man's hearts by the Creator as a norm which reason clarifies and strives to

formulate properly, and which one must always struggle to understand better, but which it is always wrong to contradict.[5]

And in the *Instruction* the same point is expressed in a complaint:

> The civil legislation of many states confers an undue legitimation upon certain practices in the eyes of many today; it is seen to be incapable of guaranteeing that morality which is in conformity with the natural exigencies of the human person and with the 'unwritten laws' etched by the Creator upon the human heart.
>
> (chap. III; pp. 37f)

THE CITIZEN'S RIGHTS

Specifically what is at issue in the making of these remarks is the view of the Magisterium that the civil law must require that the embryo or the fetus be treated as a person, or as a citizen of the state. If the state does not do so, it denies 'the equality of all before the law'; it fails to 'place its power at the service of the rights of each citizen' (*Instruction*, ch. III; p. 36).

Having the rights of a citizen means, among many other things, being protected against being treated as an object of experimentation, or being disposed of as superfluous. This is generally accepted. Warnock, for example, notes that, for the majority on her Committee of Inquiry, 'unlike a full human being, it (the embryo) might legitimately be used as a means to an end that was good for other humans'.[6] Thus, it was acknowledged that 'a full human being' should *not* be used as a means to an end for the good of others, and, by implication, that, as a citizen, this right of the human being should be protected by civil legislation. Where the Warnock majority differed from the minority, and from the perspective of the Catholic Church, was on whether the embryo is 'a full human being', a person, entitled to the status of citizenship.

But what is it which entitles human beings to this status? It was noted earlier that the Church has grounds in revelation for regarding human beings as having immeasurably more value than other creatures: broadly, the divine plan of salvation appears to be a plan for the salvation of human beings alone. No other species, it is held, is destined for 'beatific communion with God';

the special calling reserved for human persons (see *Instruction*, Introd., sect. I; p. 6). In so far as this is accepted as divinely revealed truth, then it may constitute a legitimate ground *within the faith* for singling out human beings for unique rights. But it *cannot* serve as a principle on which to base civil law, for it derives from a revelation which many do not recognise (and which, the Church concedes, has not been received by all).

Nevertheless, there are strong revelation-independent considerations which can be invoked to underwrite the special status accorded to humans in civil society. Despite the evidence of some cognitive abilities and of moral sensitiveness on the part of some other animals, none appears adapted to, or capable of, entering into a whole range of reciprocal relationships which are constitutive of the citizen-to-citizen or interpersonal bonding which cements civil society. Chief among these are legal, economic, and political relationships. If it were to transpire that some other animals were capable of entering into a broad range of these relationships, then we would be obliged to reconsider their continued exclusion from the status of persons before the law. As it is, however, there seems to be no good reason for the civil law to diverge from the revelation-based view that membership of the human species is a *necessary* condition for having the special status which attaches to personhood and, therefore, for being a potential citizen.

On the other hand, where civil law and the Christian view, at least as interpreted by the Catholic Church, does frequently diverge is on whether being a human being is a *sufficient* condition for being a person, that is, on whether *all* members of the species are to be accorded this status. The debate in this area is often muddied by the taking of 'human being' in different, and sometimes unclear, senses. Mary Warnock, for example, apparently holds the view that being 'a full human being' is what is required, and that the early embryo is not such a being, but we are not told what would constitute the requisite fullness. What is clear, however, is that to be a human being in the 'full' sense, it is not sufficient just to be a member of the species.

To be an individual of the species *Homo sapiens* might be all that is required for being a person in the *theological* sense, if it is to be believed that each and every member of the species is called to 'beatific communion' with God. However, there is no reason of similar compellingness for treating all human beings as persons *in civil law*. Many members of our species are no more capable of involvement in the range of reciprocal relationships characteristic of participation in civil society than are the non-humans which are excluded from personhood by virtue of that incapacity. In the case of humans, for some this incapacity is permanent; for others it is temporary.

The vast majority of pre-natal human beings fall into the latter category, that is, they are only temporarily incapable of participating in civil society. Civil legislation generally does not regard this incapacity as a disqualification from being treated as a person, at least in the more basic senses, such as having a right to life and a right not to be used as a means to an end for the good of others. However, there is a divergence of practice on the question whether *all* prenatal human beings are to be treated as having these rights. One commonly used criterion for marking off those who might be held to have such rights from those who might not is *viability*: if the fetus can be expected to survive independently of its mother, then it must be held to have a right to life.

The criterion is notoriously difficult to defend philosophically. Its adoption probably owes more to considerations of convenience or expediency than to its being rationally defensible. If medical science advances sufficiently to make it possible to keep a fetus alive and growing, independently of its mother, at *any* stage of its development, one wonders whether viability will continue to be regarded as the significant factor.

From a philosophical point of view, the most noteworthy development at the fetal stage is the onset of brain activity. This acquires its significance because the human brain is the organ which makes it possible for human beings to engage in the relationships characteristic of a person (one who might partici-pate in civil society). But early brain activity is merely on a level comparable with that of other animals: detection of stimuli (painful and pleasurable sensations) and response thereto (motive responses). For this reason, it could be argued that brain activity, of itself, is not the crucial development; that this lies rather in the commencement of *cognitive* activity. However, as this is difficult to date precisely, caution might dictate that, in law, the fetus ought to be treated as having attained personhood once brain activity had become established.

This approach is broadly consistent both with some recent

suggestions by secular philosophers,[7] and with a certain conjunction of trends in Catholic thought. The conjunction in mind
is that of (a modified application of) the benefit-of-the-doubt
principle coupled with the Thomistic understanding of fetal
development. The latter, as has been seen, has remained consistent from Thomas himself to the current day in the view that
personhood (ensoulment) requires, in Rahner's expression, a
'sufficient biological substratum', meaning the physical capacities necessary for exercising rationality. This stage follows one
in which the fetus had merely the animal capacities of growth,
sensation, and motion, which, in turn, was preceded by a stage
in which growth (including physical development) was its sole
capacity. As it cannot be determined accurately when the
biological substratum sufficient for personhood has developed,
but as it is clear that it must be preceded by the stage at which
sensation and motion have become possible, then it would be
groundless to postulate it earlier than that stage, and increasingly
risky to postulate it at later points. The benefit-of-the-doubt
principle, therefore, suggests that it should be postulated some-
time after the establishment of sensation and motion.

This conclusion approximates to that arrived at by Joseph
Donceel and criticised by Norman Ford. Ford contends that
Donceel's argument involves:

> the unjustified demand for the formation of sense organs and
> of the brain for rational ensoulment once it is admitted that
> there are no rational functions performed for at least two
> years.[8]

That is, he is implying that Donceel has either to accept the
'personalist' view, that there is no person until self-conscious,
rational activity begins, or to accept that a person exists once
there is an ontological individual of a human nature (from the
primitive streak stage).

What I am suggesting is that a legitimate use of the benefit-
of-the-doubt principle enables us to ride the horns of this
dilemma. While it is certain that there is a person once self-
conscious, rational activity becomes evident, and while it is
equally certain that there cannot be a (human) person in the
absence of sense organs, it is not certain at what stage in between
these poles the person comes into existence, that is at what stage
the capacity for activation of self-conscious, rational action is

attained (as opposed to becoming actually active and evident). The more advanced the fetus/early infant, the greater its claim to be given the benefit of the doubt. But only *extreme* caution, verging on scepticism, would demand unqualified treatment as a person for the fetus from the first indications of sensitive life.

THE EMBRYO/FETUS AS CITIZEN?

Recent Church teaching, however, has gone much further than this and contended that not only must the *fetus* be respected as a person at all stages of its development, but even the earlier *embryo*, from the moment of conception, must be so treated. If this is construed as an extension of the benefit-of-the-doubt principle within the framework of a Thomistic perspective, then, as was argued in the last chapter, it is an illegitimate one. The illegitimacy resides in the emptying of the notion of doubt of all factual import: there is no empirical uncertainty concerning the capacity of the embryo for rational activity; it is evident that it has no capacity of this sort. The only kind of doubt regarding what does or does not exist for which there remains 'scope' here is *sceptical* doubt; the idea that we can *never* be absolutely sure about any factual matter. But to regard such a doubt as a basis for governing action would not only be foreign to Thomism, and Catholicism, but would defeat all attempts at constructing a rational moral system, with the consequent implications for rational legislation.

Perhaps the most persuasive non-theological argument for treating the embryo as a person is the thin-end-of-the-wedge argument. If it is allowed that embryos are not citizens, that is, not persons before the law because they lack certain capacities, then, the argument goes, as time progresses, the criteria demanded for qualifying as a person might become more and more restrictive, gradually eliminating early fetuses, later fetuses, the new-born, mental defectives, and so on. Although this argument is popular with anti-abortionists, and is one which deserves serious consideration, it is virtually absent from statements of the Catholic Magisterium. The reason for this is that the current perspective of the Magisterium leaves no room for a thin end of the wedge: to kill an embryo is to kill a human being which already has rights as a person (*Instruction*, ch. I, sect. 1;

p. 14). Thus to allow IVF techniques which would result in such killings would be to permit a wedge with a *blunt* end.

To reach this position the Church has had to depend heavily on its interpretation of revelation. Indeed, the thrust of this book is that it is now reduced to relying *exclusively* on religious dogma. In due deference to its natural law tradition, an argument based on natural reasoning is retained in the *Instruction* and in the earlier *Declaration*, but, as shown in Chapter 5, this argument is hopelessly defective. The consequence of this situation for the Church's right to call for measures in civil legislation are devastating, not only from a secular point of view, but even from the Church's own traditional standpoint.

As noted earlier, the limitation which the Church finds legitimate to impose upon civil legislation is that it must not contradict 'the natural law engraved in man's hearts by the Creator as a norm which reason clarifies and strives to formulate properly'; the natural law must conform with 'the natural exigencies of the human person'.[9] This principle is an integral part of the Thomistic tradition to which the Church is heir.

A great deal of emphasis has been laid throughout this book on that Thomistic tradition. This has not been intended to suggest that Thomism is the only philosophical-cum-theological position which the Church could adopt, much less to suggest that Catholicism is wedded to the detail of Thomas' arguments or conclusions, for example, those concerning embryonic and fetal development. The point, rather, is that Catholicism has identified itself with the broad stance of Thomism, that is, with the mediation theme focused upon in the second chapter; a theme which has anti-scepticism and anti-dualism as corollaries, and which leads to the expectation that what it teaches as universal moral principles will be susceptible to support from considerations independent of beliefs derived from revelation. If it abandons that position now, it abandons both the principle which could legitimise its role as universal guardian of human rights *and*, simultaneously, the most fundamental of the characteristics which has distinguished it from Protestantism.

THE CHRISTIAN'S DILEMMA

The Protestant theologian, Nigel M. de S. Cameron, provides

an illustration of the latter point. Rejecting the charge that Christian doctrine is guilty of speciesism, he remarks:

> I hope that Christian apologists will press this deeply pagan idea into service in illustration of the illogic of the current obsession with 'human rights' – human rights conceived as natural rights as over against the human dignity which Christians have always believed to be conferred on man by virtue of his creation in the image of God.[10]

No Thomist could have written that. From the Thomist perspective, the perspective which has characterised Catholicism, there is no opposition between natural human rights and divinely bestowed human dignity. On the contrary, the view, as already noted, is that 'grace perfects nature'; it does not supplant it.

The contrast between the competing outlooks is vividly portrayed in a recent issue of the journal which Cameron edits, *Ethics and Medicine: A Christian Perspective*. Michael Bell, a lawyer, writing in the editorial comment section, observes:

> The usual approach of the pro-life movement is as follows. It recognises that we live in a world where people are less and less inclined to base their conduct on religious dogma. It therefore avoids religious dogma in its ideology, and relies on reason. It appeals to people to recognise the dignity of man, and accordingly to respect life. It argues that human dignity demands justice for the unborn child from conception onwards.
>
> The time has come to recognise that this approach is not working. . . The pro-life movement can only succeed when it recognises that we are children of God, and that therefore every human being is endowed with a unique dignity by virtue of that fact.[11]

But if the movement must rest its argument on this premiss, then it can succeed only when it has brought society at large to share in its faith. It cannot succeed with a population which does not have the Christian perspective.

Apparently by chance, the same number of the journal contains an article by S. G. Potts, presenting the case for a Thomistic approach. In doing so, Potts highlights the difficulties faced by the Bell/Cameron/Protestant perspective (without identifying it as such). He takes the view that there can be little substantial doubt about the validity of arguments against abortion based on scripture and Christian tradition, but he goes on:

> No amount of argument to the immorality of abortion from within the Christian perspective will convince one who rejects that perspective and the basic premises it involves . . .
>
> Thus a dilemma arises: the Christian who seeks to persuade his opponent of, say, the immorality of abortion, must either instil faith in him, or he must use a rational argument which forgoes all reference to faith . . .
>
> Those who find such a dilemma disturbing will take comfort from Aquinas, whose theological and philosophical work . . . is structured round the thesis that non-Christian rationality *can* yield a coherent and wholly admirable set of conclusions about how we should order our lives.[2]

Potts goes on to argue that:

> The practical implication for the Christian in an increasingly pagan world is clear . . . what the Christian must do is to forgo mention of faith and dispassionately explore those arguments with which he is faced to point out their contradictions, implausibilities and defects in reason: and, more difficult still, he is also required to justify his own position, again solely by appropriate use of the irresistible force of reason.[13]

The problem is, as Bell and Cameron appear to appreciate, that the irresistible force of reason does not irresistibly support the view that the embryo is a person from the first moment of its conception. On the contrary, from a Thomistic, non-dualistic, point of view, the ascription of person status does not make sense until at least well into the fetal stage of development. The absolutely minimal requirement for being a candidate for personhood is *individual identity*, but the pre-implantation embryo, with its potential for division and recombination, fails to satisfy even this requirement.

When this point was examined in Chapter 5, the realisation of a relatively impoverished notion of individual identity was all that was being sought; essentially nothing more than that of being *irreversibly one*. It is noteworthy that Thomas Aquinas expected a *much* richer kind of individuality for qualification as a person:

particularity and individuality are more specifically and more perfectly present in rational substances who have dominion over their actions; they are not just acted upon, like others, but act by themselves [i.e., autonomously]. . . And, therefore, among other substances, individuals of a rational nature have a special name, and this name is *person*.[14]

These remarks, which stand quite independently of Thomas' views on embryonic/fetal development, point even more firmly than the latter away from the idea that the embryo, or early fetus (or even later fetus), could be thought of as a person: autonomy is not a feature of prenatal life.

The Church, therefore, finds itself in a dilemma similar to that faced by Potts' Christian: it must either acknowledge that the teaching it offers is based on premisses taken on faith alone, or it must resort to rational argument, whose principles, as Potts says, are equally binding on Christian and pagan. If it embraces the first horn of the dilemma, the Bell/Cameron/Protestant line, then it can retain its teachings but it forfeits the ground on which it could, with propriety, demand that legislation respect those teachings, and it loses its distinctive Catholic identity at the same time. If it embraces the other horn, while it honours its tradition and retains its distinctiveness, it seems that, in the light of the deficiencies in its argument, it is compelled to modify its stance on embryo legislation in particular, and most probably on early abortion legislation too. However, the benefit-of-the-doubt argument, applied in the modified manner suggested above, could still be called upon to resist abortion after the stage at which sensation/motion capacities had established themselves.

None of this implies that the Church should have to abandon its teaching that abortion at any stage, or the destruction or experimental use of embryos, *is wrong*. As the *Declaration on Procured Abortion* points out, even if a belated animation (ensoulment/attainment of personhood) is supposed, 'there is still nothing less than a *human* life, preparing for and calling for a soul'.[15] That is to say, there is something in existence which is destined for development into personhood. To intercept that development, to frustrate that destiny is not to harm a person, for no person yet exists to be harmed, but if it is held that it was God who had destined the embryo/fetus for ensoulment, then the interception would be a defiance of the divine will.

The offence is, in significant respects, similar to the offence of artificial contraception: if artificial contraception is wrong, it is wrong because it contradicts divine designs. As the moral theologian, John Mahoney notes, all reference to the sexual faculties as designed for procreation relies heavily on a religious belief in a Creator God.[16] The calling of the embryo for ensoulment, as mentioned in the *Declaration*, can only be understood as *God's* calling of it for ensoulment. Thus there is a revelation-based argument against embryo research and abortion which is unconnected with the discussion on the timing of ensoulment/dawning of personhood.

In so far as religious beliefs about divine design are the *sole* basis of this view, then appeals for its recognition in civil law are without appropriate ground. But it is sometimes argued that, given the natural propensity of the human embryo to develop into a person, the law must respect it as it respects persons. The argument is hinted at in the quotation from the *Declaration* given above: even if the embryo is not ensouled it is still 'nothing less than a human life, preparing for and calling for a soul'. But the argument is usually not advanced in Church pronouncements. Recent documents tend to side-step the issues by proposing the view that the embryo is not a potential human being, but a human being with potential, apparently exploiting the ambiguity between 'human being' and 'person'. In any case, the Church's own teaching that ensoulment is not a natural outcome of the development of the embryo, but the result of a specific divine act, tends to undermine the potentiality argument. Given this teaching, Rosalind Hursthouse observes: 'It could not even be said that, in its earliest stages, the foetus is a potential human being, for it is not in its own nature to develop a soul'[17] ['human being' here is not, of course, being used in the purely biological sense].

JUSTICE AND EQUALITY

Even if the alleged necessity of direct divine action for the attainment of personhood is disregarded, it does not appear to be incumbent upon the legislature to protect the potentiality of potential persons. The *Response to the Warnock Report* produced on behalf of the Catholic Bishops of Great Britain, states that:

In a pluralistic society, the law's efforts and sanctions must be focused most particularly on clear cases of *injustice*. A wider effort to give legal effect to other moral principles (even true moral principles such as we believe and profess as Christians) might disrupt the community-wide acceptance and sense of fairness on which the law's defence of *justice* must in practice depend.[18]

On this basis, the *Response* goes on to propose that IVF (which is considered morally wrong) might be legally permitted within marriage, but that it should be forbidden in circumstances in which 'it will in practice inevitably involve the grave injustice of destruction of embryonic human beings'.[19]

But in what sense is the destruction of embryonic human beings an *injustice*? Upon whom is the injustice held to be inflicted? The notion that anything, or anyone, other than a citizen, or person, or rational agent, can suffer injustice is relatively recent. Historically there existed a wide-ranging consensus on the potential scope for justice and injustice. Aristotle held that:

> Justice can exist only among those whose relations to one another are governed by law, and law exists only among those who may be guilty of injustice . . . people between whom injustice is possible are capable of acting unjustly towards one another.[20]

For Kant:

> Justice is the aggregate of those conditions under which the will of one person can be conjoined with the will of another in accordance with a universal law of freedom.[21]

Even the utilitarian John Stuart Mill recognised that:

> Justice implies something which is not only right to do, and wrong not to do, but which some individual person can claim from us as his moral right.[22]

And finally, Thomas Aquinas remarks:

> As the name 'justice' implies equality, by its nature justice can obtain only between one and another . . . and insofar as it pertains to justice to govern human acts, this equality which justice requires must be between those capable of action.[23]

On none of these accounts of justice can the human embryo suffer injustice, for all deem justice and injustice to be realisable only in a situation in which there exist the requirements for a reciprocating relationship between agents.

This conception of justice does not preclude the possibility of an injustice being done by treating the embryo in certain ways, but such an injustice would be done, not to the embryo itself, but to someone who had rights regarding the embryo, e.g. a parent.

Jeremy Bentham sowed the seeds of the idea that injustice might be done to beings beyond the circle of reciprocating agents when he urged that the question to be asked concerning non-human animals is not 'Can they *reason?* nor Can they *talk?* but, Can they *suffer?*'[24] This extension of the circle has much to commend it, but it still fails to bring into the arena of possible objects of injustice the embryo and the early fetus, for the answer to the question 'Can they suffer?' is 'No'.

The reference in the bishops' *Response* to the 'grave injustice of destruction of embryonic human beings', therefore, appears to beg the question of the personal status of embryonic human beings. Such destruction, in itself, can be an injustice only if *persons* are being destroyed. Arresting a process which may eventually result in a person coming to be is not the destruction of a person, and not (in itself) an injustice, because no holder of the rights or interests necessary for suffering injustice yet exists.

In an earlier submission to the Warnock Committee,[25] the bishops' body which produced the *Response*, made it clear that they did not wish to beg the question of fetal (or embryonic) ensoulment, acknowledging that the Church has not committed itself on this question. But, immediately following this acknowledgement, the submission has the statement: 'Respect for human persons demands respect for each human being at all stages of his or her bodily life,'[26] thus implying that the timing of ensoulment is irrelevant. We are not told *why* respect for human persons demands this respect 'at all stages of his or her bodily life'; it appears to be assumed that it is self-evident.

It may be presumed that the principle is intended to be understood *distributively*, that is, that it is shorthand for the claim that respect for person x demands respect for *that* human being at all stages of x's bodily life, and that respect for person y . . . etc. We do not respect human persons *collectively*: it is not the collective that has the rights proper to persons, but the individuals. Once this is made clear, however, it transpires that the principle does not have the consequences that the bishops' body derives from it. Their problem is that at the embryonic stage we do not yet have what can properly be described as *a particular person's bodily life*. There is not yet any particular person whose bodily life it is. This is particularly evident where the embryo perishes at that stage, for then there will *never be* any particular person whose bodily life might be said to have been thus destroyed. Not only has no person suffered an injustice, therefore, but neither has any person's bodily life been lost.

But, the idea that the embryo is the bodily life of any person is problematic even in the cases where the embryo survives to grow into a mature person. Before personhood is attained, the life of the embryo or fetus is not *the bodily life of the person to be*, but *the life of the body of the person to be*. That is to say, the life of the embryo from which I grew was not a stage of *my* life, but a stage in the life of *my body*. I am not my body; I am a person, and *my* life began when the person I am came to be. The life of the embryo was a stage in the life of the body which *came to be my body* when I came to be. It cannot properly be described as 'my body' before then.

Thus, by whatever route the issue is approached, other than by appeal to revelation and divine purposes, questions concerning the requirements of *justice* do not arise (directly, that is) in connection with the treatment of the human embryo or early fetus. These questions could have a place only if it could be shown either that these life-stages were stages in the lives of persons, or that they *might be* stages in the lives of persons; i.e., that the embryo or early fetus is, or might, be a person.[27] It has been seen that not only did authoritative figures in the history of the Catholic Church think that this could not be shown (rather that the evidence pointed to the reverse), but that the anti-sceptical, anti-dualist spirit of mainstream Catholic thought, applied to the currently available scientific evidence, gives no grounds for revising that view.

On the contrary, the 'delayed animation' view, the view that it is intelligible to speak of a possible 'personal presence' only after a lapse of time (*at least* a few weeks) after fertilisation of the ovum, is strongly reinforced by current data. So strongly, indeed, that the claim that, for all we know, there *might still* be a person from the moment of conception, can continue to be maintained only within a sceptical perspective of the kind implicit in the *Declaration on Procured Abortion* when it is said that: 'it suffices that this presence of the soul be probable (and *one can never prove the contrary*)' (p. 16, n. 19 – my emphasis). As noted earlier, the reason for holding that the contrary can never be proven seems to be that the issue is held to be beyond the scope of biology, or of any other scientific or empirical investigation. But even if it is granted that this is so, the thesis of the *Declaration* stands contradicted by the Second Vatican Council statement: '[human] intelligence is not confined to observable data alone. It can with genuine certitude attain to reality itself as knowable'.[28]

CONCLUDING REMARK: RELIGION, REASON, AND CIVIL SOCIETY

One final point. In a recent publication, *Religious Convictions and Political Choice*,[29] it is argued by Kent Greenawalt that, given the limited capacity of human beings, they should not be expected to rely exclusively on rational, secular arguments in advancing views on issues such as animal rights or abortion. Even within a liberal democracy, Greenawalt holds, it is legitimate to press for respect in legislation for rights conceived on the basis of religious convictions. This is not an uncommon view outside the Catholic tradition,[30] although it is surely a deeply worrying one. It is with serious regret, therefore, that it is noted that Germain Grisez has concurred with this view. 'In the debate over abortion and public policy', he writes, 'we should hear no more charges that one party or another is trying to legislate for the whole of society on particular religious opinion. That, so to speak, is the name of the game when any serious human, moral and legal question is at issue.'[31]

That might be 'the name of the game' for those who have abandoned all hope for human reason; for those who adopt the pessimism of Luther (or, more appropriately perhaps, of Calvin) against the qualified optimism of Thomas. It is effectively to abandon the concept of natural law in its most elementary sense, that is, the notion that there is an objective moral law which careful and conscientious human thought will eventually tease into the open. It is a recipe for religious mob-rule, rather than for a society in which reasoned argument will be allowed to win the day.

Notes

1 INTRODUCTION

1. Published in English by the Catholic Truth Society, London, 1987 (all page references are to this edition: chapter and section references are provided for users of other editions).
2. A discussion of the subtleties of this issue will be found in Orsy, L. 'Magisterium: Assent and Dissent', in *Theological Studies* 48 (1987), 473–97.
3. 'Possible People', *Bioethics*, Vol. 2, (1988), pp. 279–93.
4. An inalienable right is not necessarily absolute. The force of 'inalienable' is that it cannot be forfeited or rescinded, but that does not exclude its being overridden in certain circumstances. As the inalienability of the right to life is interpreted in the *Instruction* as implying that life demands absolute respect, then it appears to be suggesting that familial rights are also being presented as requiring absolute respect, and therefore as being absolute rights. It is, of course, to be doubted if this was intended, but this serves only to accentuate the need for great precision when making statements about rights and absolute values.
5. This aspect of the document is one of the targets of Lisa Sowell Cahill and Thomas A. Scanlon in their book *Religion and Artificial Reproduction: An Inquiry into the Vatican 'Instruction'* (New York, 1988) ch. 6. For a brief critical review of their book see Benedict M. Ashley in *The Thomist*, vol. 53, (1989), pp. 153–5.
6. This has been argued elsewhere, notably by Norman M. Ford in *When did I begin? Conception of the human individual in history, philosophy and science*, (Cambridge, 1988). Ford's views are discussed briefly in Chapters 5 and 6. See further my critical review of Ford's book, *Bioethics*, vol. 3 (1989), pp. 333–41.
7. Vacek, E. V. 'Vatican Instruction on Reproductive Technology' in *Theological Studies*, vol. 49, (1988) pp. 111–31, pp. 112f. Vacek does have misgivings about the approach adopted in the *Instruction*. He remarks: 'Considering the public audience it was to receive, perhaps it should have striven to be more uplifting and positive or articulate and well-argued, but such was not its literary form' (p. 112).

2 MEDIATION AND SAINT THOMAS AQUINAS

1. Aristotle did not think that species would become extinct (or arrive by evolution), for that would be an irreparable breach in the natural order and nature can be only temporarily obstructed, never indefinitely frustrated. But these weaknesses in his biology do not vitiate his philosophical position; we could simply substitute subnuclear particles, or something of the kind, for species, and the argument would be unaffected.
2. Cf. MacIntyre, A. *A Short History of Ethics*, (London, 1971) p. 122.

3. According to Pope Leo XIII in his Encyclical Letter: '*Aeterni Patris*'.
4. See, e.g., Nelson Pike, *God and Timelessness* (London, 1970).
5. Cronin, M., 'The Moral Philosophy of St. Thomas' in C. Lattey (ed.), *St. Thomas Aquinas* (Cambridge, 1925) p. 132.
6. *Summa Theologiae*, I–II, q. 94.
7. Although it was acknowledged by the Spanish Jesuits, particularly Suarez. See John Mahoney, *The Making of Moral Theology: A Study of the Roman Catholic Tradition* (Oxford, 1987) pp. 231–43, for discussion on this point.
8. Cf. *Summa Theologiae*, vols. I–II, q. 91, a. 4, c. Thomas lists four reasons for divine law here, but only two concern the need for divine law as opposed to natural moral law. The others concern the need for divine legislation and justice arising from the limitations of human legislative power to enforce the moral law.
9. *Summa Theologiae* II–II, q. 1, a. 10, c.
10. Ibid., I, q. 1, a. 1 and *Summa Contra Gentiles*, bk IV, 76.
11. Inaugral Discourse at the Roman Academy of St. Thomas (see Lattey, op. cit. p. 32).
12. *The Documents of Vatican II*, W. M. Abbott (ed.), (London, 1966) p. 452 (*Optatam Totius*, §16).
13. Ibid., p. 452, footnote 52.
14. Gustafson, J. M., *Protestant and Roman Catholic Ethics* (London, 1979) p. 48.
15. See C. Curran, 'Catholic Moral Theology Today' in *Theological Studies*, vol. 34, (1973), and, for a more up-to-date review of recent Catholic moral theology, the concluding chapter of Mahoney, op. cit.

3 WHAT PRICE HUMAN LIFE?

1. For one of the latest critiques, see Helga Kuhse, *The Sanctity-of-Life Doctrine in Medicine* (Oxford, 1987) ch. 3. But the principle still has its defenders, for example, Campbell in R. Campbell and D. Collinson, *Ending Lives* (Oxford, 1988).
2. E.g., G. E. M. Anscombe in 'Action, Intention and Double Effect', *Proceedings of the American Catholic Philosophical Association*, vol. LVI, (1982), p. 24.
3. Reviewed by R. A. McCormick in 'Notes on Moral Theology: 1980', *Theological Studies*, vol. 42, (1981), 80ff.
4. 'La moralité des moyens', *Recherches de science religieuse*, vol. 68, (1980), pp. 205–24. Discussed in McCormick, op. cit.
5. *Humanae Vitae*, Encyclical Letter on Artificial Contraception, 1968, para. 14.
6. *Human Values and Christian Morality* (Dublin, 1970), p. 198n.
7. Cf. Thomas Aquinas, *Summa Theologiae*, II–II, 64, art. 7.
8. *Scholasticism and Politics*, (London, 1940) pp. 70ff.

4 NATURAL AND DIVINE VALUES

1. S. Kierkegaard, *Fear and Trembling* A. Hannay (trans), (Harmondsworth, 1985) pp. 98 and 101.

2. *Const. Dei Filius*, ch. 4, in Denzinger 1797.
3. Egner, G., *Birth Regulation and Catholic Belief: A Study in Problems and Possibilities*, (London and Melbourne, 1966) p. 70n.
4. For an extended treatment of this point see Egner, *op. cit.*
5. Curran, C. E., *Transition and Tradition in Moral Theology* (Notre Dame, Ind., 1979) p. 18.
6. *Summa Theologiae*, I–II, q. 94, Art. 2.
7. Egner, *op. cit.*, pp. 44f.
8. Ford, J. C., and Kelly, G., *Contemporary Moral Theology*, vol. 1, (Cork, 1958) p. 9.
9. See, e.g., *Compendium of Theology*, ch. 104–5; *Summa Contra Gentiles*, bk III, ch. 48.
10. See Kant, I., *Critique of Practical Reason*, Part I, Book II, ch. II.
11. E.g., Cronin, M., 'The Moral Philosophy of St. Thomas' in Lattey, C. (ed.) *St. Thomas Aquinas* (Cambridge, 1925) pp. 133ff.
12. Porter, J., 'Desire for God: Ground of the Moral Life in Aquinas', *Theological Studies*, vol. 47, (1986), pp. 48–68, 49.
13. E.g., J. Fuchs, *Human Values and Christian Morality* (Dublin, 1970) p. 14.
14. Karl Rahner, in *Hominisation* (London, 1965), struggles to reconcile this doctrine with a plausible evolutionary theory. His proposed solution is that the soul is to be regarded as a product of the parents' self-transcendence after all, but this self-transcendence is rendered possible only by the power of God 'immanent in their causality' (p. 99). In so far as such intervention can be described as immediate, this solution still implies a supernatural event. In so far as it is not immediate, then it fails to meet the requirements of the doctrine.
15. It is sometimes said that those who are in these extreme circumstances cannot be said to be *human* beings. This response merely underlines the need to define 'human' here. In a purely *biological* sense of 'human' they are undoubtedly human, that is, they are members (albeit handicapped or damaged ones) of the biological species *Homo sapiens*. On the other hand, if 'human' is to be taken to imply having capacitites for cognitive and moral activities, then not only these individuals, but a great many other members of the biological species *Homo sapiens* will not be human either.
16. As does, for example, Peter Singer, in his *Practical Ethics* (Cambridge, 1979).

5 THE ARGUMENT OF THE *INSTRUCTION*

1. *Summa Theologiae*, I, q. 29, a. 1.
2. *The Documents of Vatican II, Gaudium et Spes*, Art. 51.
3. See B. Haring, *Medical Ethics* (Slough, 1974) p. 76.
4. Grisez, G., *Abortion: The Myths, The Realities, and the Arguments* (New York, 1970) p. 416.
5. *Ibid.*, p. 416. For a spirited defence of Boethius' definition against recent criticism see Peter Simpson, 'The Definition of Person: Boethius Revisited', *The New Scholasticism*, vol. LXII, (1988), pp. 210–20.

6. Ibid., p. 306.
7. Ibid., pp. 418f.
8. *When did I begin?*, pp. 66ff.
9. Ibid., pp. 77 and xvi.
10. Ibid., p. xv.
11. Ibid., p. 77.
12. Ibid., p. 87.
13. 'Abortion, Animation, and Biological Hominisation', in *Theological Studies*, vol. 36, (1975), pp. 305–24, 309.
14. Not explicitly, perhaps; but implicitly, e.g., when, on the one hand, 'human' and 'person' are regarded as coextensive terms, and, simultaneously, 'being ensouled' is treated as synonymous with 'being a person'.
15. K. Rahner, *Hominisation: The Evolutionary Origin of Man as a Theological Problem* (London, 1965) p. 94.
16. For this I rely largely on the contributions of Simon Fishel and Robert Winston at the ICUS Conference, Washington DC, November 1986. Fishel's paper has since been published as: 'Human In-vitro Fertilisation and the Present State of Research in Pre-embryonic Material', *International Journal on the Unity of the Sciences*, vol. 1, (1988), pp. 173–214. Additional guidance was received from the scientific referee for the journal *Bioethics*, in which much of this chapter appeared under the title ' "From the Moment of Conception. . .": The Vatican Instruction on Artificial Procreation Techniques', in vol. 2, (1988), pp. 294–316.
17. On the first point, see R. G. Edwards, 'Test-tube babies: the ethical debate' (*The Horizon Lecture*), in *The Listener*, 27 October 1983, pp. 10–14. The second point was made by the *Bioethics* scientific referee (see note 16).
18. It will be evident that I reject the view of T. W. Hilgers (one who has disputed the evidence for natural recombination) who contends: 'If it [recombination] does occur, it would only occur extremely rarely, and then only as the result of abnormal, diseased development. Such occurrences should not form the basis of moral decision-making', ('Human Reproduction: Three Issues for the Moral Theologian' in *Theological Studies*, vol. 38, (1977), pp. 136–52, 151). Recombination would be no more a diseased development than identical twinning; the fact that it occurs less frequently is irrelevant. Further, what forms the basis of the Magisterium's moral guidance here is not the physical phenomena but the ascription of a soul to the embryo. If that ascription finds itself in insoluble difficulty in giving a coherent account of recombination, then it needs to be reconsidered.
19. Colleagues have suggested this, and it is also advanced by Michael Lockwood (in *Moral Dilemmas in Modern Medicine* Oxford, 1985, p. 160ff.) in disputing the significance attached by the Warnock Committee to primitive streak formation.
20. *Warnock Dissected*, Life pamphlet (Leamington Spa, 1984).
21. Ibid., p. 13.
22. *Abortion and the Right to Live*, Joint Statement by the Catholic Bishops of Great Britain, 21 January 1980, Catholic Truth Society, London 1980, Para. 12. and reiterated in their evidence to the Warnock Committee, *In Vitro Fertilisation: Morality and Public Policy*, Catholic Media Office, London (undated), and again in their *Response to the Warnock Report*, published by

the same office. The claim is also to be found in the *Declaration on Procured Abortion* where there is quoted the view of Tertullian (c. 200 AD): 'The one who will be a man is already one' (Para. 5). See Chapter 6 for observations on this.
23. Op. cit., p. 319. Diamond's source for this information was: J. T. Lanham, *American Journal of Obstetrics and Gynaecology*, vol. 106, (1970), p. 463.
24. Ibid., pp. 219f.

6 DOUBT AND SCEPTICISM

1. *An Essay Concerning Human Understanding*, Book II, ch. 27, §9.
2. *Practical Ethics* (Cambridge, 1979) ch. 6. Also, J. Glover, *Causing Death and Saving Lives* (Harmondsworth, 1981) chs 11 and 12.
3. *Beginning Lives* (Oxford, 1987) pp. 103ff.
4. Denzinger 2327 (quoted in Rahner, *Hominisation*, op. cit., p. 94).
5. Harmondsworth, 1955, p. 248.
6. *Cours de Philosophie*, 1910 et seq., abridged and translated as *A Manual of Modern Scholastic Philosophy*, 2 vols., (London, 1916).
7. Ibid., vol. I, pp. 318f.
8. 'Immediate Animation and Delayed Hominisation', *Theological Studies*, vol. 31, (1970), pp. 76–105, 82.
9. *Summa Theologiae*, Ia. q. 76, a. 3 ad 3.
10. E.g. by G. Grisez, *Abortion: The Myths, the Realities, and the Arguments* (New York, 1970) p. 283. This claim is also implied in the *Statement of the Catholic Archbishops of Great Britain* published under the title *Abortion and the Right to Live* by the Catholic Truth Society (London, 1980) §§11 and 12.
11. Donceel, loc. cit., draws attention to both these points. The original references are: *Theologia moralis*, vol. 3 (Bassani, 1779), tract. 4, no. 394, p. 159, and *Collectanea de prop. fide*, 1, (Rome, 1907) no. 282, p. 92.
12. See P. Badham, 'Christian Belief and the Ethics of In-vitro Fertilisation', *International Journal of the Unity of the Sciences*, vol. 1, (1988), pp. 157–71, 166.
13. See G. R. Dunstan, 'The Moral Status of the Human Embryo: a Tradition Recalled', *Journal of Medical Ethics*, vol. 1, (1984), pp. 38–44, 42f.
14. Quoted in C. A. Tauer, 'Probabilism and the Early Embryo', *Theological Studies*, vol. 45, (1984), pp. 3–33, 30f (from Donceel, op. cit. p. 89). Original reference: *Catechismus Romanus ex decreta Concilii Trid. et Pii quinti jussu primum editus* (Louvain, 1662) p. 36.
15. Ford, op. cit., pp. 58ff. See also pp. 194ff., n. 57.
16. Tauer, op. cit., p. 18.
17. Ibid.
18. Pius XII, Address to an International Congress of Anaesthesiologists, November 1957 (*AAS* 49, 1957: 1031 and 1033) – as reported by C. E. Curran, *Transition and Tradition in Moral Theology* (Notre Dame, 1979) p. 200.
19. Tauer, op. cit., p. 33.
20. See, e.g. M. Lockwood, (ed.), *Moral Dilemmas in Modern Medicine*, (Oxford, 1985), pp. 23 and 29.

21. *Corpus Christi*, bk I, p. 103 (1.31–36).
22. Loc. cit., §12.
23. Cf. Dunstan, op. cit., pp. 39ff.
24. Loc cit.
25. J. J. Diamond, 'Abortion, Animation, and Biological Hominization', *Theological Studies*, vol. 36 (1975), pp. 305–24, 322.
26. *Summa Theologiae*, Ia. q. 118, a. 2 ad 2.
27. Op. cit., p. 94.

7 REVELATION AND LEGISLATION

1. *A Question of Life* (Oxford, 1985) p. xvi. The introduction did not form part of the report itself, but was added for the benefit of readers of the Blackwell edition.
2. *Gaudium et Spes*, §74.
3. Ibid., §75.
4. Cf. *Declaration*, §20; *Instruction*, pp. 35f.
5. *Declaration*, §21.
6. Ibid., p. xv.
7. Michael Lockwood, for example, writes: 'The question of when a human being comes into existence is really the same question as that of what constitutes the identity of a human being over time: the so-called problem of personal identity', and he argues that, 'What sustains human identity is a continuity of organisation within a continuously existing brain', op. cit., pp. 14 and 29. (Note that Lockwood uses 'human being' in a more restrictive sense than that of member of the species, but this does not affect the consonance of the thrust of his argument, that is, in its implications for the treatment of the fetus.)
8. Ford, op. cit., p. 52.
9. *Declaration*, §21, and *Instruction*, pp. 37f.
10. 'Image in Embryo' in David C. Watts (ed.) *Creation and the Christian Response to Warnock* (Rugby 1985) pp. 3–12, 6.
11. 'Comment: Human Dignity?', *Ethics and Medicine: A Christian Perspective*, vol. 4, no. 2, (1988), pp. 18f.
12. 'Persuading Pagans', Loc. cit., pp. 28f.
13. Ibid., p. 29.
14. *Summa Theologiae*, I, q. 29.
15. n. 19.
16. *Bioethics and Belief*, p. 13.
17. *Beginning Lives* (Oxford, 1987) p. 32.
18. Catholic Media Office (London, undated) p. 8.
19. Ibid., p. 9.
20. *Nicomachean Ethics*, Book 5, ch. 6, J. A. K. Thomson (trans) *The Ethics of Aristotle* (Harmondsworth, 1953).
21. *The Metaphysical Elements of Justice*, 230, John Ladd (trans) Indianapolis, 1965).
22. *Utilitarianism*, ch. V.
23. *Summa Theologiae*, II–II, q. 58, art. 2.

24. *The Principles of Morals and Legislation* (New York, 1948) ch. 17.
25. *In Vitro Fertilisation: Morality and Public Policy.*
26. Ibid., p. 8.
27. Or, if Bentham's lead is followed to its conclusion, if it could be shown that they can *suffer.*
28. *Gaudium et Spes*, sect. 15. The passage continues: 'though in consequence of sin that certitude is partly obscured and weakened', Thus, *despite* the acknowledged effects of sin, the Council held that it was still possible for us to attain certitude even about matters beyond the scope of the empirical sciences, which presumably means certitude in matters of philosophy and morals.
29. (New York, 1988).
30. That is, outside of the Catholic tradition *in teaching*; it is recognised, of course, that Catholic *practice* has frequently not been faithful to the teaching.
31. *Abortion: The Myths, the Realities, and the Arguments*, p. 353.

Bibliography

BOOKS AND ARTICLES

Anscombe, G. E. M., 'Action, Intention and Double Effect', *Proceedings of the American Catholic Philosophical Association*, vol. LVI, (1982), pp. 12–25.

Aristotle, *Nicomachean Ethics* J. A. K. Thomson trans., as *The Ethics of Aristotle* (Harmondsworth, 1953).

Ashley, B. M., Review of L. S. Cahill and T. A. Shannon, *Religion and Artificial Reproduction* (see below), *The Thomist*, vol. 53, (1989), pp. 153–5.

Badham, P., Christian Belief and the Ethics of In-vitro Fertilisation', *International Journal of the Unity of the Sciences*, vol. I, (1988), 157–71.

Bell, M. N. M., 'Comment: Human Dignity?', *Ethics and Medicine: A Christian Perspective*, vol. 4, (1988), 18–19.

Bentham, J., *The Principles of Morals and Legislation*, (New York, 1948).

Cahill, L. S. and Shannon, T. A., *Religion and Artificial Reproduction: An Inquiry into the Vatican 'Instruction on Respect for Human Life in its Origin and on the Dignity of Human Reproduction'* (New York, 1988).

Cameron, N. M. de S., 'Image in Embryo', in C. Watts (ed.), *Creation and the Christian Response to Warnock*, Biblical Creation Society pamphlet, Rugby, 1985.

Copleston, F. C., *Aquinas* (Harmondsworth, 1955).

Cronin, M., 'The Moral Philosophy of Saint Thomas', in C. Lattey (ed.), *Saint Thomas Aquinas* (Cambridge, 1925).

Curran, C. E., 'Catholic Moral Theology Today', *Theological Studies*, vol. 34, (1973).

Curran, C. E., *Transition and Tradition in Moral Theology* (Notre Dame, 1979).

Diamond, J., 'Abortion, Animation, and Biological Hominisation', *Theological Studies*, vol. 36, (1975), pp. 305–24.

Donceel, J., 'Immediate Animation and Delayed Hominisation', *Theological Studies*, vol. 31, (1970). pp. 76–105.

Dunstan, G. R., 'The Moral Status of the Human Embryo: a Tradition Recalled', *Journal of Medical Ethics*, vol. I, (1984), pp. 38–44.

Edwards, R. G., 'Test-tube babies: the ethical debate', *The Horizon Lecture*, *The Listener*, 27 October 1983, pp. 10–14.

Egner, G., *Birth Regulation and Catholic Belief: A Study in Problems and Possibilities* (London, 1966).

Fishel, S., 'Human In-vitro Fertilisation and the Present State of Research in Pre-embryonic Material', *International Journal on the Unity of the Sciences*, vol. I, (1988), pp. 173–214.

Ford, J. C. and Kelly, G., *Contemporary Moral Theology*, vol. 1 (Cork, 1958).

Ford, N. M., *When did I Begin? Conception of the Human Individual in History, Philosophy and Science* (Cambridge, 1988).

Fuchs, J., *Human Values and Christian Morality* (Dublin, 1970).

Glover, J., *Causing Death and Saving Lives* (Harmondsworth, 1981).

Greenawalt, K., *Religious Convictions and Political Choice* (New York, 1988).

Grisez, G., *Abortion: The Myths, the Realities, and the Arguments* (New York, 1970).

Gustafson, J. M., *Protestant and Roman Catholic Ethics* (London, 1979).

Hare, R. M., 'Possible People', *Bioethics*, vol. 2, (1988), 279–93.

Häring, B., *Medical Ethics* (Slough, 1974).

Hilgers, T. W., 'Human Reproduction: Three Issues for the Moral Theologian', *Theological Studies*, vol. 38, (1971), pp. 136–52.

Hursthouse, R., *Beginning Lives* (Oxford, 1987).

Kant, I., *Critique of Practical Reason*, L. White Beck (trans), (Indianapolis, 1956).

Kant, I., *The Metaphysical Elements of Justice*, J. Ladd (trans), (Indianapolis, 1965).

Kierkegaard, S., *Fear and Trembling*, by A. Hannay (trans), (Harmondsworth, 1985).

Kuhse, H., *The Sanctity-of-Life Doctrine in Medicine* (Oxford, 1987).

Life (Save the Unborn Child), *Warnock Dissected* (pamphlet) (Leamington Spa, 1984).

Locke, J., *An Essay Concerning Human Understanding* (A. D. Woozley edition, London, 1971).

Lockwood, M., *Moral Dilemmas in Modern Medicine* (Oxford, 1985).

McCormick, R. A., 'Notes on Moral Theology: 1980', *Theological Studies*, vol. 42, (1981), pp. 74–121.

MacIntyre, A., *A Short History of Ethics*, (London, 1971).

Mahoney, J., *Bioethics and Belief: Religion and Medicine in Dialogue* (London, 1984).

Mahoney, J., *The Making of Moral Theology: A Study of the Roman Catholic Tradition* (Oxford, 1987).

Maritain, J., *Scholasticism and Politics*, (London, 1940).

Mercier, Cardinal, and Professors of the Higher Institute of Philosophy, Louvain, *A Manual of Modern Scholastic Philosophy* (London, 1916).

Mill, J. S., *Utilitarianism* (M. Warnock edition, London, 1969).

Orsy, L., 'Magisterium: Assent and Dissent', *Theological Studies*, vol. 48, (1987), pp. 473–97.

Pike, N., *God and Timelessness* (London, 1970).

Porter, J., 'Desire for God: Ground of the Moral Life in Aquinas', *Theological Studies*, vol. 47, (1986), pp. 48–68.

Potts, S. G., 'Persuading Pagans', *Ethics and Medicine: A Christian Perspective*, vol. 4, (1988), pp. 28–29 and 32.

Rahner, K., *Hominisation: The Evolutionary Origin of Man as a Theological Problem* (London, 1965).

Shannon, T. A., see Cahill, L. S.

Simpson, P., 'The Definition of Person: Boethius Revisited', *The New Scholasticism*, vol. LXII, (1988), pp. 210–20.

Singer, P., *Practical Ethics* (Cambridge, 1979).

Thomas Aquinas, *Summa Theologiae* (Marietti edition, Taurini, 1928).

Thomas Aquinas, *Summa Contra Gentiles* (Marietti edition, Taurini, 1927).

Tauer, C. A., 'Probabilism and the Early Embryo', *Theological Studies*, vol. 45, (1984), pp. 3–33.

Vacek, E. V., 'Vatican Instruction on Reproductive Technology', *Theological Studies*, vol. 49, (1988), pp. 111–31.

Warnock, M., *A Question of Life: The Warnock Report on Human Fertilisation and Embryology* (Oxford, 1985).

PRINCIPAL CHURCH DOCUMENTS

The Documents of the Second Vatican Council, W. M. Abbott (ed.), (London, 1966).
Humanae Vitae, Encyclical Letter on Artificial Contraception (Pope Paul VI), 1968 (St Paul Editions).
The Declaration on Procured Abortion, Congregation for the Doctrine of the Faith, 1974 (now published under the title *Let Me live*, Catholic Truth Society, London, 1983).
Abortion and the Right to Live, Catholic Archbishops of Great Britain, 1980 (published by the Catholic Truth Society, London, 1980).
In Vitro Fertilisation: Morality and Public Policy, Submission to the Warnock Inquiry on behalf of the Catholic Bishops of Great Britain, Catholic Media Office, Abingdon (undated, but c. 1983).
Response to the Warnock Report, on behalf of the Catholic Bishops of Great Britain, Catholic Media Office, Godalming (undated, but c. 1985).
Instruction on Respect for Human Life in its Origin and on the Dignity of Procreation: Replies to certain questions of the day, Congregation for the Doctrine of the Faith, 1987 (published by the Catholic Truth Society, London).

Index

abortion, 7, 26, 65, 79, 86, 105, 106, 111
Abraham, 42–3
agent, rational/reciprocating, 108–9
Alphonsus Liguori, 86–7
animals, non-human, 9, 49–50, 56, 91–2, 98–9, 109; *see also* speciesism
animation, 65, 74, 84–5, 106, 110–11; *see also* ensoulment
Anscombe, G. E. M., 114
Aristotle, 11, 13–15, 18, 50–1, 108, 113
Ashley, B. M., 113
Augustine, 13, 17–18, 20, 21, 45, 68, 86
autonomy, 59, 106

Badham, P., 117
Barth, K., 13
Bell, M., 104–5, 106
Bentham, J., 109, 119
Billot, Cardinal, 24
biological identity, *see* identity
Boëthius, 59, 61, 64, 80–1, 115
brain-death, 91

Cahill, L. S., 113
Calvin, 16, 20, 43, 111
Cameron, N. M. de S., 103–6
Campbell, R., 114
capital punishment, 27, 37–40, 48
citizen, as legislator, 1, 3; as subject, 45; rights/status of, 98–103, 107–8
cleavage, cell, 69, 84, 95
cloning, 71
Collinson, D., 114
common good, 40, 45, 97
Conception, Immaculate, 86–8
conception, the moment of: at implantation, 76; and biological discontinuity, 94–5; ensoulment from, 72–4, 86, 87–8, 90–1; a person from, 7, 8, 78–9, 81, 96, 102,

110–11; right to life from, 3, 35, 54, 58–9, 60
conjugal act, unitive and procreative meanings of, 5–6, 26, 47–9
consequentialism, 30, 31, 35, 37
contraception, 5–6, 26, 30, 46–9, 107
Copleston, F. C., 83
Cronin, M., 114, 115
Curran, C., 48, 114, 115, 117

Descartes, 21
Diamond, J., 66, 76, 94, 117, 118
Donceel, J., 85, 101, 117
double-effect, 27, 28–35, 36, 39
doubt, benefit of the, 77, 78–92, 96, 101, 102, 106
dualism/anti-dualism, 9, 19, 21, 82–3, 96, 103, 105, 110
Dunstan, G. R., 117

Edwards, R. G., 69, 116
Egner, G., 115
embryo dormancy, 75–6
embryo, human: as ensouled, 71–4, 81–8, 89–92, 116; as individual, 63, 68–74, 76; as person/human being, 7–8, 57, 58, 64–77, 105; as potential person/human being, *see* potentiality; treatment of, 2, 6–7, 8–9, 26, 46, 58, 78–80, 86, 98, 102–3, 106–7, 108–11
embryo research, 11, 26
embryology, 10, 69–71, 84–5, 95–6
ensoulment: and biological development, 67–8, 71–4, 82–5, 94–5; and personhood, 9, 17–20, 59–60, 71, 116; timing of, 58–9, 60, 81, 86–7, 89–90, 106, 109–11; *see also* immediate creation
equality, 108
evolution, 55, 67, 68, 113, 115

fertilisation/procreation, artificial, 4–7, 57, 66; *see also* *in vitro* fertilisation

fetus: development into, 70, 73;
  ensouled and unensouled, 86–7,
  94; and justice, 108–9, 110; as
  person, 9–10, 56, 80, 98, 100–3,
  105
Fishel, S., 116
Ford, J., 50, 115, 117, 118
Ford, N., 62–4, 80, 88, 101, 113
Fuchs, J., 36–7, 39, 48, 115

gene therapy, 69
genetic identity, *see* identity
genetic discontinuity, 66–7, 94
Glover, J., 117
Greenawalt, K., 111
Grisez, G., 8, 61–2, 111, 115, 117
Gustafson, J. M., 114

Hare, R. M., 4
Häring, B., 115
Hilgers, T. W., 116
human being: constitution of, 115,
  118; dignity of, 7–8, 35, 54, 56–7,
  89, 91, 98–100, 105; embryo as, 58,
  76–7, 98–9, 102; and person, 7–8,
  9–10, 60–4, 71, 80–1, 107, 108–9,
  116; potential, 74, 96
Hursthouse, R., 81, 107
hylomorphic theory, 18–20, 81–2, 85

identity: biological, 65, 66, 68;
  genetic, 66–7, 69, 74–5; individual,
  65, 71, 72, 75, 93, 105–6; personal,
  9, 72, 73–4, 93–4, 118
immediate creation (of the soul), 54,
  55, 58, 82, 93, 107, 115
implantation, 70–1, 75–6
in vitro fertilisation, 4, 6–7, 11, 26, 79,
  103, 108
individual identity, *see* identity
individuality, 19, 62–4, 68–74, 82, 106
insemination, artificial, 4, 6; *see also*
  fertilisation, artificial
innocence, 57
Isaac, 42

Jesus Christ: conception of, 87–8;
  divine incarnation in, 12, 15
John Paul II, Pope, 69

justice/injustice, 38, 39, 104, 107–10,
  114

Kant, I., 38, 51–2, 56, 108, 115
Kelly, G., 50, 115
Kierkegaard, S., 43, 114
Kuhse, H., 114

Lanham, J. T., 117
law/legislation: civil, 1, 2–3, 6, 7, 9–
  10, 11, 16, 44–5, 63, 97–103, 106,
  108, 111–12, 114; divine, 22, 42–5,
  46, 54, 114; eternal, 22; natural,
  11, 12, 16, 20–3, 24, 25, 26, 44–53,
  54, 56, 97, 103, 111, 114
Leo XIII, Pope, 23, 114
liberal democracy, 111
Locke, J., 62, 80
Lockwood, M., 116, 117, 118
Luther, 11, 15–16, 21, 43, 111

McCormick, R. A., 114
MacIntyre, A., 113
Magisterium: authority of, 1–2; and
  civil legislation, 8, 98; and moral
  law/theology, 48–9, 50, 55; and
  natural law, 44, 46, 55; and the
  Pauline principle, 29–30; and the
  potentiality argument, 74, 93–4;
  and the timing of ensoulment, 58–
  9, 86–7, 89–91, 116
Mahoney, J., 107, 114
Maritain, J., 40
marriage, 2, 3, 5–6, 26, 46–7, 108
mediation, 3, 11–17, 23, 24, 83
Mercier, Cardinal, 23–4, 83–5, 86, 90
Mill, J. S., 108
murder, 78–9

natural law, *see* law
natural science, 21, 23
nidation, *see* implantation

obsequium, 2
Orsy, L., 113
ovum, fertilised, 65, 69, 71, 73, 93, 110

Paul VI, Pope, 5, 24, 25, 30, 31, 44,
  46, 55

Paul, Saint, 29–30
Pauline principle, 28–35, 37, 46
person: as citizen, 98–103; concept of, 7–8, 14, 18, 59–64, 80–5, 105–6; embryo as, 9, 64–71, 76–7, 78–9; and ensoulment, *see* ensoulment and personhood; potential, 93, 96, 107–8; respect due to, 7–8, 9, 38, 109–10
personal identity, *see* identity
Pike, N., 95
Pius IX, Pope, 86
Pius XII, Pope, 55, 82, 117
Plato, 11, 13–14, 17–18, 20
pluralistic society, 108
Porter, J., 53, 115
potentiality, 74–6, 92–6, 107
Potts, S. G., 104–6
primitive streak, 70, 101, 116
probabilism, 89–92
procreation, artificial, *see* fertilisation
proportionality, principle of, 20, 83, 85, 92
Protestantism, 3, 10, 11, 12–13, 43, 103–4, 106
public policy, 2, 7, 8, 61; *see also*, law, civil

Rahner, K., 68, 96, 101, 115, 116
revelation, divine, 8, 12, 15, 22, 44, 54–5, 98, 103
revealed law, *see* law, divine
right to life, 2, 3–4, 7, 59, 100, 113
rights: absolute *v.* inalienable, 3–5, 113; of the child, 3–5, 6; of the family, 2, 3, 22, 113

Scanlon, T. A., 113
scepticism/anti-scepticism, 9, 21, 88–92, 96, 102, 103, 111
Schüller, B., 29
Schweitzer, A., 50
self-defence, 3, 28–9, 30–1, 48
Simpson, P., 115
Singer, P., 80, 115
situation ethics, 24–5

soul: and body, 9, 17–20, 21, 81–5; and embryonic development, 71–4, 79, 116; and evolutionary theory, 67–8, 115; immortality of, 19, 51–2, 67; nature of, 13–14, 59; *see also* ensoulment
speciesism, 49–56, 59–60, 61–4, 80–1, 98–100, 104
Suarez, E., 114
surrogate motherhood, 2, 4, 6

Tauer, C., 89, 91, 117
Tertullian, 93, 96, 117
thin-end-of-the-wedge argument, 102–3
Thomas Aquinas: and Aristotelianism, 14; and double-effect, 28; and embryology, 85-6, 92, 95–6, 105–6; and legislation, 45, 108, 111; and natural law, 11, 20–3, 47, 49; psychology of, 17–20, 50–3, 59, 81–2; thought of, 3, 10, 15–17, 23–5, 83, 103
Thomism: and Catholic higher education, 23–4; and embryology, 89, 92, 95, 101, 105; and epistemology, 83, 102; and psychology, 81–2, 84–5, 87–8; and the reformers, 15, 43; the tradition of, 103
totipotential, 70, 71, 72–3
Trent, Council of, 16–17, 23, 85
twinning, 66, 70, 71–3, 116

Vacek, E. V., 113
Vatican Council, First, 23, 43–4
Vatican Council, Second, 24, 54, 55, 60, 97, 111
viability, 100

Warnock, M., 97, 98, 99
Warnock Committee/Report, 71, 97, 107, 109, 116
William of Ockham, 43
Winston, R., 116

zona pellucida, 70, 72–3
zygote, 66, 94